CHRONIC PAIN
The Complete Guide to Relief

Also by Arthur C. Klein with Dava Sobel

Arthritis: The Complete Guide to Relief
Arthritis: What Really Works
Arthritis: What Exercises Really Work
Backache: The Complete Guide to Relief
Backache: What Exercises Really Work

CHRONIC PAIN

THE COMPLETE GUIDE TO RELIEF

Arthur C. Klein

CARROLL & GRAF PUBLISHERS, INC.
New York

Carroll & Graf Publishers, Inc.
19 West 21st Street
New York
NY 10010-6805

First published in the UK by Robinson,
an imprint of Constable & Robinson Ltd 2001

First Carroll & Graf edition 2001

ISBN 0–7867–0834-4

Printed and bound in the EU

*For my Mom,
a woman
of inestimable courage*

For my wife, Pat, with love

For John J. Halperin, MD, with gratitude

Contents

Foreword

Chronic pain is a complex physical and psychological state associated with numerous medical diagnoses including chronic low-back pain, osteoarthritis, peripheral neuropathy, cancer, chronic headache and facial pain, myofascial pain, fibromyalgia, spinal cord injury, stroke, complex regional pain syndrome (Types 1 and 2), degenerative joint disease and osteoporosis. When chronic pain follows an injury, it does not become "chronic" until after a sufficient time has passed to allow the body to heal normally. The time of normal body healing is variable and depends on many factors including the type of injury, the body region involved and the age of the injured person. The physical/medical processes responsible for the initial pain, e.g. the active viral infection associated with shingles, or a recently herniated disc in one's lower back, may no longer be active for someone with chronic pain. However, an explosion of scientific information regarding the mechanisms of chronic pain over the past decade or so has allowed all involved in the evaluation and treatment of chronic pain to appreciate and understand much more clearly why people continue to experience pain even, for example, after the medical problem is "fixed." Without adequate treatment, chronic pain can lead to a vicious cycle of disability, dysfunction, depression, anxiety, fear, illness conviction and an overall deterioration in the quality of one's life.

Not infrequently, the precise cause of an individual's chronic pain problem cannot be determined despite exhaustive and extensive diagnostic testing. Often, this particlar circumstance leads to the diagnosis of "psychogenic pain," a diagnosis that,

99.9 per cent of the time is completely medically and scientifically inappropriate. For example, most people who experience hyptertension, despite years of scientific research which has been completed to better understand its causes, do not have a known, defined cause of their elevated blood pressure. When was the last time someone with high blood pressure was labeled as having a psychogenic process? When was the last time someone with elevated blood pressure was told to go home and just live with it—without any guidance (medical, lifestyle change or exercise) regarding management of the problem? By not recognizing chronic pain as a distinct affliction with multiple causes, some of which we can determine and many of which we cannot, the medical profession, in general, has not been fair to individuals who suffer from it. Often people who suffer from chronic pain are forced to spend the majority of their time justifying their pain—I cannot recall the last time a person I was working with had to justify their diabetes to me.

Chronic pain is not a rare phenomenon. More than 90 million Americans are affected by a chronic, not cancer-related, painful condition which often results in a disruption of work-related, social and family activities. The cost, in dollars, in human suffering, and in economic loss from both treatment and long-term disability is overwhelming. In the United States alone, the prevalence of chronic pain during the 1980s was estimated to be 97 million persons, resulting in 68 million disabled Americans, 702 workdays lost, all at a total estimated cost of $68 billion. *Chronic pain disables more Americans and costs more to the United States of America than the combination of cancer and heart disease combined!*

A unique aspect to chronic pain is the diversity of disciplines that care for people who suffer from it as well as those who contribute to pain research efforts. Neurologists, anaesthesiologists, surgeons, physiatrists, psychiatrists, psychologists, physical and occupation therapists, neuroscientists, pharmacists, chiropractors, nutritionists, acupuncturists, vocational counselors, to name a few, all play important roles in the management and research of chronic pain.

The book that you are about to read, *Chronic Pain: The*

Complete Guide to Relief, has been written by Art Klein to help those individuals suffering from chronic pain to begin, and hopefully complete, a journey "From Pain to Life". As Klein emphasizes over and over again, in a clear and stepwise fashion, human beings that must endure chronic pain can become more active and functional again. By acknowledgment of the fact that no available treatment can guarantee complete and permanent resolution of a person's chronic pain and by consistently highlighting the role of increasing physical activity in combination with other medical and non-medical approaches, Klein points out how essential it is that the individual suffering from chronic pain becomes an active, responsible participant in the treatment and management of his or her pain. This point cannot be emphasized enough, in my experience, as the field of pain management has become increasingly technologically and pharmacologically oriented, chronic pain sufferers have often become discouraged and disgusted when their pain persists despite treatment. Klein helps the reader to remember that medical and even non-medical treatments are tools to help *reduce* pain and facilitate activity but not necessarily to cure and obliterate the pain forever. Acceptance of this process is one of the major themes of this book and certainly a key to living successfully with chronic pain.

Charles E. Argoff, M.D.,
Co-Director, Cohn Pain Management Center,
North Shore University Hospital

1

From Pain to Life: The Journey Starts Here

Please take a journey with me that will change your life for ever. Our journey together will glow brightly with hope, love, empathy and caring – and with a proven and simple way for you to recover from chronic pain.

This is a world where:

- an invisible global epidemic is disabling hundreds of millions of lives
- pain is the only constant and reality, yet patients are often told there's nothing *really* wrong with them
- no major study on chronic pain has ever been conducted
- medical schools worldwide devote less than one half of 1 per cent of their general curriculum to chronic pain
- most physicians have little or no training in chronic pain management
- the real experts, for the most part, are *not* healthcare professionals, but thousands of individuals who have successfully turned their lives around – chronic pain sufferers who have managed to break the deathly grip of long-term pain.

On our journey, we'll discover a new body of knowledge that explains, step by step, how certain individuals suffering from chronic pain got well.

This new information I have gathered from two surveys that I have conducted, and from a decade of dialogue with individuals with varying levels of pain and incapacitation – and I hope it will provide you with a springboard to recovery. It works no matter how many practitioners and treatments you've tried. No matter how many times you've made the rounds. No matter how discouraged you feel. No matter how limited your life may be. It works because it is based on how individuals like you and me have dramatically improved their lives. They got well. And so can you.

2

You Can Get Well Even If You are Filled with Doubts

When you've been in pain for a long time, despite having tried a variety of treatments, it's normal to feel skeptical, isolated, angry and despairing.

The good news is that these negative feelings are to be expected. They are normal. Indeed, if you still felt optimistic or happy after years of pain, incapacitation and failed treatments, your mental health would be questionable! The key point to bear in mind is this: your negative feelings will not prevent you in any way from getting well!

You can recover from chronic pain regardless of how long and difficult a road you've travelled. The content of this book is based on the recoveries of more than 1,000 chronic pain sufferers who saw an average of ten healthcare practitioners – deriving little or no help from any of them – and with negative results from about a quarter of them.

You can recover from chronic pain whether or not you have a diagnosis. The diagnosis, "Chronic Pain Syndrome," should be commonplace, but it isn't. Medical schools now recognize Chronic Pain Syndrome. Current medical textbooks consider Chronic Pain Syndrome a disease in itself. And yet most healthcare providers are still in the dark about it.

IT DOESN'T MATTER WHAT YOUR CHRONIC PAIN IS CALLED

Do not be concerned with the name given to your chronic pain. If you have been thoroughly examined by at least two competent physicians, have taken every relevant medical test, and there is still *no known physical basis* for the pain that you have suffered for two or more months, then you have, by definition, Chronic Pain Syndrome.

Here's one example of Chronic Pain Syndrome. You once had acute pain from a low-back strain. The strain is now healed. Yet your pain is rampaging, progressive, intractable – meaning, it hurts like hell, nothing seems to make it better and there is no end in sight.

Similarly, if your pain from a *known physical origin* greatly exceeds the so-called norm for a particular ailment, you have Chronic Pain Syndrome. Let's say, for example, that you have osteoarthritis. You've taken every manner of medication for it, both over the counter and prescription. You've tried physical therapy, exercise and other treatments. Yet, your pain persists at a level greater than can be explained by healthcare practitioners. To recover, you would need to be treated for both osteoarthritis *and* Chronic Pain Syndrome.

CHRONIC PAIN BY ANY OTHER NAME

Have you received a diagnosis that is simply another name for chronic pain? No doubt you have. Here are just a few of the hundreds of possible diagnoses:

- "nothing really wrong"
- chronic low-back syndrome
- chronic neck pain
- strain or sprain of back or neck
- myopathy or neuropathy
- degenerative disc disease
- misalignment
- pinched nerve
- subluxation
- chronic bulging disc
- stress
- psychogenic pain.

YOU'RE NOT ALONE

In the long run, the most painful aspect of chronic pain is

feeling alone with it, feeling that there is no end in sight. You see yourself as the patient no one wants to deal with because a full battery of medical tests have produced no definitive answers. You have to endure the dismissive and blaming attitude of medical doctors who have no training in chronic pain management and no compassion for your distress. You feel that you're the patient who is under suspicion simply because Chronic Pain Syndrome isn't taken seriously or diagnosed for what it is.

Every single one of the more than 1,000 recovered chronic pain sufferers whose input contributes to this book used to be alone with their pain. Their hearts are with you. I am one of these recovered chronic pain sufferers. My heart is with you.

YOUR DOUBTS – AND YOUR COURAGE – ARE THE KEYS TO YOUR RECOVERY

There has never been a human being with chronic pain who didn't have painful doubts and questions. Could I have figured out some way to prevent this horrible condition from ever occurring? Did I push myself too much and bring on chronic pain? Why are other people with similar pain origins functioning well, and why am I not? Am I exaggerating my pain? Do I complain too much about it? Am I lacking in courage? Am I being unfair to my family? Shouldn't I just be able to grit my teeth and go on?

There is a simple answer to such questions. *Chronic pain is a disease. It is no more your fault than a broken leg, blood poisoning or cancer*. Think of it this way: given the hostility you tend to encounter in connection with chronic pain, and the lack of answers available, it is no small miracle that you are still alive and trying.

Think about the statement: "Your doubts – and your courage – are the keys to your recovery." How can your doubts about this book's recovery plan – or any other approach to recovery – possibly help you? Skepticism is essential. It gives you the potential power to stay away from dubious treatments. It enables you to pick your way through the minefield of bad advice about chronic pain. It might even help you to keep a bit of your sense of humour. Your doubts can help preserve your sanity!

Your courage also is to be commended and not to be taken lightly. Most people who are ill know exactly what is wrong with them; you don't. Most are not in constant pain; you are. Most have both a diagnosis and a prognosis. You've lived day in and day out without having a precise diagnosis or specific treatment plan. It takes great courage to face constant pain, and the unknown, at the same time. Accept your courage as a given if you can, and give yourself credit for the bravery it takes to live with chronic pain.

Because you're reading this book, you have what it takes to try to get well. Take this courage with you on our journey, and use your doubts to say, "I will give the next step a try. If that step works, I'll take another step." We will proceed, one step at a time, toward your recovery. Help *is* on the way.

3

An Overview of this Book's Success Plan

Did the recovered chronic pain sufferers surveyed for this book have anything in common other than making it back to health?

The 1,000 individuals, all of whom overcame the ravaging effects of chronic pain after years of uninterrupted suffering, relied on the **five steps to success** that form the basis of this book. These five steps give you the essential tools you need to improve your life, including knowing how to find the right kind of professional help when it is needed.

All five steps are:

- easy to understand and follow
- designed with minimal risk and gradual, lasting progress in mind
- proven effective by individuals like you.

Here is a summary of each of the steps, and how they can help to change your life:

STEP 1 OVERCOMING ISOLATION, SELF-BLAME AND DESPAIR

This step was covered in chapter 2, but here is a quick summary. You are not alone with your pain. You are not to blame for your pain. And, most assuredly, you can get well no matter how skeptical and despairing you may feel.

STEP 2 SORTING OUT MYTHS THAT HARM FROM TRUTHS THAT HEAL

When you live with chronic pain, you encounter a world of well-meant advice from strangers, friends, relatives and healthcare practitioners. Myths and misinformation of all kinds – whether about attitudes or treatments, diagnostic tests or herbal miracles – can cause confusion and conflict and make it more difficult to recover.

Much of the advice that you get about chronic pain is incorrect or harmful. The point of this step, then, is to arm you with knowledge, clarity and the truths you need to set yourself free from a life of chronic pain.

STEP 3 SUCCEEDING PHYSICALLY: THE BODY–MIND RECOVERY PLAN

With all the hype today about "mind–body" and why does this book emphasize a "body–mind" recovery plan? In brief, because it works.

When you have suffered pain unceasingly for months or years, and have seen a variety of healthcare practitioners with poor results – and when there is little or no hope in sight – it's the most difficult time of all to be positive and to learn sophisticated mind–body techniques.

It makes more sense to start your recovery with tangible, physical steps forward that lift your spirits and give you reasons to be hopeful. Of course, mind–body energy matters. And, yes, using your mind to direct your body in a positive way is essential and necessary for a full and productive life. But, mind–body techniques aren't the *initial* key to success for most chronic pain sufferers, especially when it can take months or years to master techniques such as meditation, guided imagery and self-hypnosis. It is better, at the outset, to take simple and effective physical steps. These physical steps will, in turn, almost instantly, help produce the positive mental energy you need to enhance your physical progress.

In just a few weeks of following this book's Body–Mind Recovery Plan, you can expect to see substantial if not dramatic results. You'll be able to do more each day. You are likely to feel less pain with each passing day and week.

The Body–Mind Recovery Plan is based on these simple but effective principles:

- GUARANTEED FIRST-STEP SUCCESS. "Guarantee" is a word that publishers and attorneys dread. But I use it here for good reason. The first activity that you perform, in either a walking or swimming programmeme, will be at a level that is 20 per cent *less* than what you know you can do right now on your very worst days. Can you do 20 per cent less than the worst you've ever done? Yes, you can! And that first taste of success will get you going in the right direction.
- GRADUALISM. This means moving forward stage by stage, a step at a time, in an orderly way. Think of it as taking baby steps that quickly become longer strides, and then giant steps. Or, think of it as rehabilitation – more progress each day until you are fit once again. The opposite of gradational is what we'll call "ups and downs" – an approach to recovery that ends in failure every time. Most of us who have suffered chronic pain, and I include myself in this group, have unintentionally taken the "ups and downs" route – days of stepped-up activity followed by days of increased pain and diminished activity. Doing more than we can, then having to cut back.
- MIND–BODY ACTIVITIES THAT YOU *ALREADY* KNOW AND LOVE. We're not talking fancy techniques here, but simple pleasures that you may have neglected or dropped since chronic pain came into your life. Examples: prayer, reading a novel, listening to music, watching comedy videos or visiting a loved one.
- INVOLVING OTHERS. Briefly explaining your recovery plan to the people closest to you is one way of involving others. Talking to a "Plan Buddy" every day for just a minute or two, to report on your progress, is another way of reaching out and feeling less isolated and more supported.

STEP 4 ACCELERATING PROGRESS:
HOW TO BE YOUR OWN CHRONIC PAIN EXPERT

You can quickly become your own best chronic pain expert in the following ways:

- *Learning an effective stretching and strengthening programmeme that tones you up, helps you to look and feel better and gives you more zest for progress and for life.* The exercises in this book represent the first simple programme based on the success-through-exercise experiences of recovered chronic pain sufferers themselves. Unlike typical fitness "no-pain-no-gain" exercises, these take a "do-no-harm" approach. They are simple. They are conservative. And they work.
- *Finding a number of small but highly important ways to make your daily life more comfortable and active.* You'll learn how to observe yourself throughout the day – and pick up valuable cues for making your life better. You'll find dozens of helpful tips – from getting out of bed to vacuuming, from putting on shoes to finding easier ways to garden, from finding the best sitting positions to discovering the least stressful and most enjoyable sexual-activity positions.
- *Taking simple actions to relieve pain.* Learn:
    * how to stop pain before it starts
    * how to use the "pink-thumb" technique to halt localized pain
    * what the best over-the-counter painkiller is
    * why using heat and ice in combination is often the best idea of all
    * how to deal with acute pain that mixes with your chronic pain

and many other self-help techniques.

STEP 5 GETTING EXTRA HELP: A GUIDE TO WHAT
WORKS AND WHAT DOESN'T WORK

Would professional help be useful? Is the doctor you're working with a good bet? If not, how do you choose a new doctor? Who are the best-rated kinds of practitioners for chronic pain? Who are the worst? Which diagnostic procedures are unnecessary and which can harm you? Does acupuncture work? Chiropractic treatment? Percutaneous electrical stimulation? Mind–body strategies? Multidisciplinary pain centres? This book is a uniquely practical guide – with clear answers based on the input of more than 1,000 recovered chronic pain sufferers – to what works and what doesn't work for chronic pain.

4

Medical Myths and Truths

When we live with chronic pain for months or years or decades, we tend to *become* that pain. Pain is the haze before our eyes – a numbing murkiness that fills our bodies, our minds and our lives. Pain makes it difficult to think clearly about anything, including a way out of pain.

We see the best healthcare practitioners we can find. But, with each passing diagnosis and prognosis – no two alike – our confusion can grow. Each practitioner has something different to say. We don't know what to think. As the months and years pass, the myths and misinformation pile up. With so many conflicting approaches and opinions to cope with, it's easy to feel like quitting.

The point of this chapter, then, is to help you become clear about the facts of chronic pain. To help you sort out medical myths from medical realities. Once you grasp these realities, these truths, you'll automatically feel more empowered. More than anything else in this book, the truths that you learn about chronic pain can arm you, defend you and set you on the path to wellness.

Most myths about chronic pain originate with doctors. Some of these myths are misguided. Others are seemingly belligerent. All ultimately make it more difficult for chronic pain sufferers to get well.

MYTH: "THERE'S NOTHING REALLY WRONG WITH YOU."

Pretend for a moment that *you* are a physician. A chronic pain sufferer comes in to see you. He says, "I'm in pain . . . there's something really wrong with me."

What would you say? Nearly 90 per cent of chronic pain sufferers are told by one or more practitioners: "There's nothing really wrong with you."

Why this blatant disregard of a patient's reality? The answer is a simple if painful one: because doctors don't know precisely what causes or prolongs chronic pain, they have two choices. They can say that you have chronic pain, even though they don't understand its origins as well as they would like. Or they can send you on yet another ride into despair by saying, "There's nothing really wrong with you." Such a statement or response is morally reprehensible. It is destructive. It is *really wrong*. The fact that you're there in the doctor's surgery, the fact that you're hurting – no matter what role your mind or body may be playing, no matter what the source or origin of your pain – means that something *is* really wrong.

Chronic pain is, by definition, ongoing pain whose cause is unknown. It is as real as pain caused by what we *do* know and as deserving of compassion and the best efforts at treatment as any other kind of pain. To deny an individual's pain is to desecrate his dignity. If we are to live in a humane world, calling relentless pain "nothing wrong" is a form of cruelty and demonstrates a lack of care that must be banished from doctors' language and thought.

What can you say if a doctor tells you "there's nothing really wrong." You can remind yourself, indeed you *must* remind yourself, that there is something wrong. To the doctor, you can say, "Clearly, there *is* something wrong or I wouldn't be here seeing you. It would be far kinder for you to say, 'I don't know what is wrong, but I accept the reality of your pain and I care about it.' Also, it would be far more professional for you to know that, according to current medical teachings, ongoing, long-term pain of an unknown origin *is* something; it's called chronic pain and should be taken as seriously as any other disease."

MYTH: "NO ONE EVER DIED OF CHRONIC PAIN."

People do die from chronic pain. The numbers aren't known, precisely because chronic pain has yet to be treated as a disease worth major research funding.

It is known that people who have relentless pain for more than a few days get down about it. It is known that long-term pain causes despair and depression. It is known that a sense of hopelessness can make us sick. It is known that incapacitation is bad for the body and mind. It is known among doctors who treat long-term chronic pain that suicide is a risk, and sometimes a reality.

Chronic pain can kill and the cruelty of saying "No one ever died of chronic pain" should be grounds for loss of a healthcare license. It betokens a coldness and lack of awareness that is unacceptable from a member of the caring professions.

MYTH: "YOUR CHRONIC PAIN SYMPTOMS HAVE NO MEANING."

Doctors who say that your symptoms of *chronic* pain have no meaning, value, consistency or purpose are incorrect. What are they missing here? They are using *acute* pain as their model. With acute pain, there is obvious value to pain. Acute pain tells you not to touch a flame, to get help for your broken leg, to look into that pain in your stomach.

But, when acute pain goes on for months, and cannot be traced to a physical origin, some prominent physicians who head up pain centres believe that these symptoms are meaningless and without value. These physicians are quick to point out that they *do* believe the pain exists, but they feel that the symptoms no longer tell us anything useful.

Survey participants for this book feel that this theory of chronic-pain-symptoms-without-value is based on medical arrogance. They believe that individual differences in pain matter; they matter to the individual and they matter to the treatment and they wonder how anyone could think otherwise. I believe that, some day, the symptoms of chronic pain will be better understood. For the moment, these symptoms must be heeded, respected and treated as caringly and effectively as possible. As the great dancer, Martha Graham, once said: "The body never lies." We must dig harder to discover the body's truths about the symptoms of chronic pain.

MYTH: YOU HAVE ACUTE PAIN OR CHRONIC PAIN – NOT BOTH

Search the world's medical databases, read every medical textbook ever written, and you are unlikely to find one word about treating the simultaneous conditions of chronic pain *and* acute pain.

Tell the average doctor that you have chronic pain – and acute pain – and he or she is likely to question your sanity. Yet this undiagnosed condition – a merger of chronic pain and acute pain – exists in almost every instance of chronic pain.

If you're suffering from chronic pain, your muscles are more likely than normal to be susceptible to acute pain. In other words, when you're not in great shape, you're more apt to strain something bending over. Or pull a muscle sneezing! Or suffer pain from doing more than you're accustomed to.

For the most part, healthcare practitioners have no understanding of this condition. They've never thought about it or worked out a strategy for trying to help patients with it. So, what can you do right now about the intermingling of chronic pain and acute pain? Quite a bit!

You'll find many practical tips for easing both acute pain and chronic pain in chapter 9, "Instant Relief: The Best and Safest Non-Prescription Pain-Stoppers."

MYTH: "STRESS IS A LARGE PART OF YOUR PROBLEM."

It used to be thought that ulcers were caused by stress. Never mind that there were tens of millions of other people suffering from stress, without ulcers. And never mind that there was no reliable research proving that stress caused ulcers. The always-fashionable stress was said to be the cause. However, there is no clinical evidence that stress causes ulcers. Today, we can pinpoint ulcer-causing bacteria that eat away at our stomach linings and can be treated with antibiotics.

"Stress" is too often the garbage-heap of unrefined and undocumented medical diagnoses. If we don't know what is causing a medical problem, and we're too filled with pride to use three simple words – "I don't know" – then we unscientifically assign stress as the underlying cause of medical conditions.

Is stress the cause of chronic pain? Is it fair for a doctor to say, "There definitely seems to be an element of stress underlying your condition?" What if anything is known about the relationship of stress to chronic pain? Let's take these questions one at a time.

There is no scientific data supporting the theory that stress causes chronic pain. And logic dictates otherwise. If stress causes chronic pain, and all human beings suffer stress, then all of us would be in chronic pain.

It used to be assumed that stress caused back pain. The reasoning went like this: when you're under stress, your muscles tense up, and tense muscles can lead to spasming and overall physical pain. Sounds good, admittedly. But the only scientific medical research ever conducted about low-back pain and stress, as reported in the *New England Journal of Medicine*, says otherwise. This research tells us that stress has nothing to do with our ability to predict who will, and who will not, suffer back pain.

What should your reaction be, then, if a practitioner says, "Stress seems to be playing a role in your chronic pain?" Or, "Stress appears to be causing you greater pain?" The response depends on the doctor's tone and intent. If the words are said with compassion, "Let's see what we can do for the stress that chronic pain causes, and give you some relief," that would be helpful. Or, if the words are said in a kind manner, "It could be that stress is making your chronic pain worse, and perhaps we can work together to give you some relief," that would be of real value. If, on the other hand, the suggestion is made, either in tone or words, that stress *caused* your chronic pain, or that you somehow caused your stress, tell that practitioner that the *cause* of chronic pain is unknown and that you're going elsewhere.

Some 70 per cent of this book's survey participants believe that stress makes their pain worse. But not a single person believes that stress *caused* their chronic pain. For certain, where there is chronic pain, there is stress. But this stress is the result of, not the cause of, chronic pain. Stress is *not* the pain sufferer's fault. It is one of the given outcomes of chronic pain. In other words, it is simply impossible to be human, and to suffer pain for a long time, and not have stress from it.

There are many specific steps that you can take to ease stress. Please see chapter 12, "Mind–Body Healing," for details.

MYTH: "THERE IS A PSYCHOGENIC COMPONENT UNDERLYING YOUR CONDITION."

This bears a similarity to the preceding myth, but it's worth a separate mention. *Psychogenic* refers to a medical condition – pain in this case – that starts in the mind. For example, you're in anguish over something in your life and that mental anguish turns into ongoing physical pain.

Medical research, however, does not bear out this theory for the average pain sufferer. Unless the diagnosis of a "psychogenic component" is made by a qualified psychiatrist or psychologist who has thoroughly tested and evaluated you, it's a wild guess at best, blaming and dismissive at worst.

MYTH: "SECONDARY GAINS MUST BE AT WORK HERE."

The theory here is that there are benefits to having chronic pain – and that these benefits are pleasing enough to be worth your pain and suffering. For example, if you're unhappy in your marriage because you don't get the attention you think you deserve, and your pain gets you more attention, you would be enjoying "secondary gains".

There is little evidence in medical literature that secondary gains play a significant role in creating or perpetuating chronic pain. It is *never* justified for any medical practitioner to make this diagnosis without extensive psychiatric or psychological training.

MYTH: "YOUR DESCRIPTION OF YOUR PAIN SYMPTOMS IS UNCLEAR OR INCONSISTENT; THEREFORE YOU MUST BE IMAGINING OR EXAGGERATING YOUR PAIN."

This myth is as ignorant of the realities of chronic pain as fifteenth-century theories about sailing off a flat earth.

Chronic pain isn't the same from day to day. This makes it frustrating, if not impossible, for a chronic pain sufferer to describe his or her symptoms clearly. Indeed, there are often so many symptoms, that vary from hour to hour, or from day to day, that someone uninformed about chronic pain could easily believe that there are hundreds of millions of people spending their days inventing oddball symptoms.

If you cannot describe your symptoms precisely, it isn't your fault; it's simply the nature of chronic pain. No matter how extensive your vocabulary, no matter how articulate you may be, it is impossible to assign words to chronic pain in a way that precisely pinpoints that pain.

MYTH: "YOU DON'T HAVE CHRONIC PAIN. WHAT YOU HAVE IS LOW-BACK PAIN, OSTEOARTHRITIS, MISALIGNMENT, A PINCHED NERVE, DEGENERATIVE DISC DISEASE, BONE SPURS, IDIOPATHIC LUMBAR-SACRAL RADICULOPATHY, MYOSITIS, NEUROPATHY, MYOPATHY, FIBROMYALGIA, CHRONIC MYOFASCIAL PAIN SYNDROME, YIN–YANG IMBALANCE, ENERGY BLOCKAGE OR ANY OTHER OF DOZENS OF DIAGNOSTIC TERMS."

Although current medical literature views chronic pain as a disease in itself, the word about this accepted view has not spread to the vast majority of healthcare practitioners. This means, sadly, that if you have chronic pain, you are highly unlikely to get a diagnosis of chronic pain. Instead, you'll get one of the diagnoses listed above.

How can you pick your way through this rabbit warren of diagnostic chaos? You can give yourself a diagnosis of chronic pain if:

- You have been thoroughly examined by two or more highly qualified medical doctors. Every conceivable test has been run. Every avenue of disease and malfunction has been looked at. And there is no known cause for your day-in, day-out pain lasting three months or longer.
- Your constant pain from a known cause – osteoarthritis, for example – exceeds the normal range of pain to be expected from that disease.
- You get different diagnoses from different specialities and there is no scientifically demonstrable, provable reason for your pain. For example, suppose that you have had back and leg pain for more than three months. A good internist and a good neurologist have examined you from head to foot. You've had a blood analysis. Perhaps you've also had an MRI or a CT Scan. Nothing can be found. Yet, you're told by an orthopedic surgeon that you have a bulging disc; you're told by a chiropractor that you have subluxation; you're told by an osteopath that you have misalignment; you're told by a primary-care physician that you have low-back syndrome.

MYTH: "THERE ARE NOW CENTRES AND CLINICS DESIGNED SPECIFICALLY TO SOLVE CHRONIC PAIN PROBLEMS."

There are centres for the treatment of pain. But no two pain centres are alike and few follow the same model for staffing and treatment. For example, there are pain centres that work primarily with medications, and pain centres that seldom, if ever, use medications. There are pain centres where the psychological factors are considered, and pain centres where the psychological is ignored. There are pain centres headed up by anaesthesiologists, by neurologists, by physiatrists and by orthopedists.

Some pain centres are helpful for chronic pain. Generally, though, they are working with too little knowledge, too little training and too few pain experts to reverse the trend of chronic pain as a leading cause of suffering and disability.

MYTH: "EVERYTHING THAT CAN BE DONE FOR YOU HAS BEEN DONE. YOU'RE JUST GOING TO HAVE TO LEARN TO LIVE WITH THIS."

This is almost never true. Why? Because most healthcare practitioners have so little training in chronic pain management, they aren't qualified to sentence you to a life of pain or hopelessness.

However, there is one small kernel of truth about "learning to live with this." It could well be that you're going to have to take charge of your own case more actively. You're going to have to do more for yourself. Ultimately, that's what this book is about – learning how to play a greater role in taking charge of your life, and of your recovery from chronic pain.

5

General Myths and Truths

What are the five worst things about chronic pain? In the opinion of the recovered chronic pain sufferers who participated in this book, they are:

1. The pain itself.
2. The uncertainty about whether and when you will get well.
3. The lack of a specific diagnosis. "Chronic Pain Syndrome" is rarely used as a diagnosis in spite of its theoretical acceptance by the medical profession as a disease in itself.
4. The differing advice and opinions that virtually everyone has about chronic pain.
5. The difficulty in sorting out facts from fallacies.

It is painful, to say the least, to live with the uncertain outcome of chronic pain and, on top of that, to have to tolerate wildly diverse opinions about what's wrong with you and what you should do about it.

Anecdotal tales of "magic-bullet" cures come at you from every direction. Not that you ask people for their advice – it comes with the territory. If you do ask for advice, you'll get it beyond what your mind can absorb. Ask a thousand strangers about chronic pain, you'll get a thousand different answers, and need to live to be a thousand to pursue all of them.

Here are some of the anecdotes, myths and unsupported miracles you're likely to encounter. Here, too, are the facts and truths you must be armed with in order to keep your sanity and save your time and money.

MYTH: "I KNOW SOMEONE WHO HAS PAIN JUST LIKE YOURS. HE/SHE WAS ALMOST INSTANTLY CURED BY_____."

No two pain sufferers have the same symptoms. So, no, it isn't true that the person you're speaking to knows someone who has chronic pain just like yours. You can dismiss this fallacy every time!

As for second-hand reports of instant cures, they're almost never correct because chronic pain rarely has a single or a quick solution. I heard about one such cure at a point in my life when I had been bedridden for three years, and my then-wife and I were expecting our first child. The timing was right. I was desperate enough to listen to anything. My wife knew a nurse who knew a doctor who reputedly had a 100 per cent cure rate for virtually any kind of muscular pain. That sounded good so we set up an appointment, without first checking the doctor's credentials or asking for the names of a few of his patients who would be willing to talk to us. This doctor may well have been the only orthopedist in the world who believed that all muscular pain originated from "unstable joints." His solution was to stabilize the joints by injecting the pain sufferer with a solution that deliberately created scar tissue around joints, thereby "stabilizing" them. I received thirteen injections up and down my spine on my first and only visit to this doctor. The result? If I thought I had been in pain before I went, and I had been, now I *really* knew what blinding pain felt like. It took three months before I could lean my back against a chair without wincing. Six months after these injections, when I received a CT scan at New York's Hospital for Special Surgery, a noted orthopedist from this medical centre approached me, with a sad face, to tell me that I might have tumors running up and down my spine. It turned out that he was looking at scar tissue from my injections – more scar tissue, in more places, than he had ever seen.

MYTH: "CHRONIC PAIN? I HAVE PAIN, TOO. EVERYONE DOES. BUT, AT LEAST YOU DON'T HAVE ANYTHING SERIOUS."

A lot of survey participants in this book lied about their diagnoses when friends and acquaintances asked them what was wrong. It was unbearable to them to be out of work and have their lives fall apart because of "low-back pain" or "lumbar strain" or other innocuous-sounding diagnoses. It just didn't sound like much of anything. It didn't sound serious enough. People would regard them as wimps. One medical doctor who participated as a layperson in this book's survey, a fifty-year-old woman who had to retire from her position in a major hospital because of chronic pain that originated as post-operative scarring, used to tell people that she had "a rare and fatal neurological disease." In her words, "At least that scary diagnosis kept everyone off my back about what was wrong with me."

Of course, it's true that everyone *does* have pain at times. For most people, it comes and goes. They can live their lives in spite of it. But chronic pain is as different from these "occasional aches and pains" as cancer is from a benign tumor.

This may make it sound as if it's difficult to keep your wits about you and preserve your sanity when you have chronic pain, and it is. That's why, as part of your recovery, it's helpful, if not critical, to have the feeling that you're understood. Just about anyone can play this role – a friend, a family member, your doctor, a psychologist. Whatever it takes, try to find this compassionate support. It's dispiriting, to say the least, to feel in pain *and* to feel misunderstood and alone.

MYTH: "MAYBE YOU'VE JUST GOT TO GRIT YOUR TEETH AND GET PAST IT."

If you could "just get past it", and not be slowed down or disabled by chronic pain, of course you would! The suggestion that you bite down on a bullet and battle your way through chronic pain belittles your efforts and downplays your disease. It's like suggesting to someone with a broken leg that he's not trying hard enough to sprint. It is condescending because it assumes that you're not already fighting with all your heart and soul to be fully able-bodied.

Survey participants for this book unanimously reported feelings of doubt about themselves at some point in their illness. It is easy to feel down about yourself when you're in pain from morning to night. I remember once getting so furious with someone who compared her pain to mine – she had backache after gardening too much – that I said, "If you woke up one day, and you were me for just one hour, and had my pain, you would understand that our situations were very different." That wasn't the most tactful thing to say, but it indicates the enormous frustration, the toll it takes, when chronic pain isn't taken seriously.

MYTH: "THERE MUST BE AN ANSWER."

I've interviewed more than a thousand pain sufferers over the past fifteen years, and nearly every one of them mentioned how bothered they were by people saying, when there *were* no answers at that time, "there must be an answer."

It's almost comical. You say, "I've been out of work for eight months with pain in my hips, and I've been to twelve different practitioners and no one has an answer for me." The reply, which might even come from your best friend, or from someone who really cares about you is, "There must be an answer." It can make you feel stupid – after all, if there is an answer, why can't you think of it? It can make you feel angry – you've been everywhere and tried everything.

As difficult as it is not to take "there must be an answer" personally, it's important to try. Understanding *why* people use the phrase can help. According to 98 per cent of this book's survey participants, people have difficulty knowing what to say to someone who has chronic pain. It's easy to know what to say to someone who has acute pain that will gradually ease and go away. You send a get-well card. You call and express sympathy. You call again and get a good progress report. And soon the misery is over.

With chronic pain, most people stop calling after a while. Seeing a life go downhill, understanding that there are no answers at the moment for the sufferer, is disturbing. Whether people love you or not, they tend to want to distance themselves from this discomfort, rather than face the disturbing reality that sometimes there are no answers.

I had an inspiring conversation about this subject a few years ago with my mother. She was eighty-five at the time, and had suffered chronic pain for some twenty years, with no answers, no solutions, nothing that worked especially well for her. She was crying as we spoke on the phone, and she said, "There must be an answer." I felt so bad for her. I was in good health at that time. And my answers for my own mother were of fleeting value. She felt horribly depressed. Her sobs grew louder. "Mom," I said, "You're an incredibly courageous person. You live every day, knowing deep down, I think, that there aren't always answers." I stopped, worried I had gone too far. Maybe I had made her feel worse. "You know," she said, "you're right. Sometimes there are no answers, but I do know that one answer is having someone like you who understands. That helps!" Her spirits had lifted. So, maybe, although there often are no answers in the traditional sense, understanding someone can at least provide a small dose of comfort.

My mother is now eighty-eight, and orthodox approaches to her chronic pain still do nothing for her. Recently, in frustration, grasping at straws, she stopped all her medications and, wouldn't you guess it, she is now walking better and feeling less pain. What *does* work for my mother? The joy of seeing family members, getting out of the house, eating a special meal, being with my dad. Love and joy work for her, to be sure.

For a more extensive evaluation of how different treatments work for chronic pain, please see chapters 9 and 15.

MYTH: "I KNOW SOMEONE WHO GOT WELL BY USING MIND OVER MATTER."

If someone knows you have chronic pain, and tells you about someone who managed to conquer pain comparable to yours by using his mind effectively, what should you feel? That you have a weak mind that could be strengthened? That your chronic pain would disappear if you had a better mind? That you should try to find a mind–body expert?

Most survey participants in this book who were told about the magic of using a mind–body approach to chronic pain felt like shooting themselves. Instead, why not consider the possibilities of mind–body strategies? Read more about them in this book. Read other books. Speak to experts in the field. And then determine whether you find any of dozens of approaches worth pursuing. Also keep in mind that a mind–body approach may be worth a try, but that relatively little is known about exactly how to tap the power of the mind to help chronic pain. The world of mind–body healing is filled with self-appointed gurus, respected researchers and people who really have little knowledge. So, be interested but maintain a healthy skepticism. (This topic is discussed further in chapter 12.)

MYTH: "TAKE RESPONSIBILITY FOR YOUR PAIN."

Of course, you need to take responsibility for your pain. But when you've lived with pain for years, and someone flips a phrase at you about taking responsibility – perhaps because you've been complaining about a doctor who couldn't help you – it's difficult to resist the temptation to punch that someone! It's also difficult to resist blaming yourself.

Try to keep a cool head. There are at least four ways of interpreting the possible meaning and relevance of the phrase, "Take responsibility for your pain."

1. The phrase might simply be meant as a truism about illness and about life in general. If so, thank the person who mentioned it and remind her or him that you feel more responsible for your chronic pain condition than anyone can imagine, and that you sometimes take responsibility to the point of blaming yourself!
2. The phrase might imply that you want others to be responsible for your condition, and that you are therefore not taking enough initiative yourself, not doing as much thinking and research as you might. If so, give yourself an honest appraisal. We all want others to solve our problems

for us. Indeed, it is almost impossible *not* to want outside help. If you think you've been leaning too far in that direction, then assuming more responsibility for your recovery is a good idea.

3. The phrase might be hostile – accusative or blaming. You might be doing everything in your power, and a damn good job at that, to guide yourself to wellness. If this is the case, just thank the person for mentioning it, or explain how much you're doing on your own.

4. The phrase might be just that – a phrase, one used by someone who has never suffered a long-term illness, or who is clueless about the huge responsibility that illness entails, or who is at a loss about what to say to you. Remember that many people are frightened by your chronic pain disease – maybe they fear they could get it themselves – and they use popular, clichéd phrases in the remote hope that they will be giving you something of value.

MYTH: "CAN'T YOU JUST TAKE A PAINKILLER?"

This is an inevitable question in a world dominated by media claims of instant pain relief for every ailment. Some doctors believe there is virtually no pain, including chronic pain, that can't be dealt with successfully by the right analgesic (painkiller). But only five of this book's survey participants found a highly effective painkiller – over-the-counter or prescribed, taken orally or administered by a patch or pump – that they could take on a daily basis without being slowed up physically or mentally.

MYTH: "HAVE YOU CONSIDERED TRYING _____? I'M TOLD IT CAN PROVIDE SOME HELP FOR ALMOST ANY KIND OF PAIN."

This statement is different from the instant-cure myth referred to earlier in this chapter. In this kind of situation, someone is advising you to try a specific treatment that *might* do you some good. Or it might be harmful. Let's take a quick look at some of the suggestions you might be hearing. You'll find further details on some of these treatments in chapter 15.

Acupuncture. It works about half the time for a wide range of ailments, including chronic pain, and gets the best results when combined with other therapies.

Aromatherapy. Better that you take a walk and smell the flowers.

Chinese herbal remedies. No known effectiveness for chronic pain.

Chiropractic (manipulation plus other therapies). Varies by the skill of individual practitioners. Some success, but rarely on breakthrough levels.

Faith healing. Faith can heal, but don't lose faith if it doesn't! The best faith healer is probably the one inside your own mind and spirit.

Fitness training. Trendy in some pain rehabilitation centres, but not recommended for its "no-pain, no-gain" approach.

Glucosamine/Chondroitan. Medical research has shown that this combination of substances works best for knee pain brought on by osteoarthritis.

Gravity inversion. Relaxing, but don't let its reputed therapeutic value (or your blood) go to your head.

Homeopathic remedies. Worth looking into, especially for arthritic-based chronic pain.

Increased hydration (drinking more water). The theory goes like this: the more water you drink, the more wastes get carried away from your muscles. If you want to try drinking eight tall glasses of water each day, it might do you some good generally. But, theory aside, hydration has no known value for chronic pain.

Magnet therapy. There is no widely accepted proof that magnets have more value than a placebo, but they do help some people with joint and muscle pain.

Manipulation. Relied on by millions. Some value for long-term pain when treatments are given regularly.

Massage. Not much more than soothing, except for neck pain.

Mind–body strategies. The range of outcomes varies from frustration to transformation.

Posture therapy. Can be a helpful adjunct to other therapies.

Pyramids. Hokum that once had its fifteen minutes in the health-media spotlight. It was thought by many people that having any pyramid shape in a room with them had a curative effect and that the pyramid shape itself emitted a healing power.

Rolfing. This very deep massage technique is too painful for the vast majority of chronic pain sufferers.

Shiatsu. Recommended more for relief from acute pain.

Yoga. As a mental and spiritual discipline, combined with ever-so-gentle exercises, Yoga can work wonders.

6

Finding the Starting Level that is Right for *You*!

Congratulations! You're at the starting line of the Body–Mind Recovery Plan. You soon will take your first physical step toward success. When you do, you will immediately start to tap into your own resources of body–mind and mind–body energy. Hope will glimmer brighter.

With all the hype today about "mind–body", why is this book emphasizing a "body–mind" recovery plan? Because, without a single exception, survey participants for this book liked the idea of starting recovery with tangible, physical steps forward that lifted their spirits. Mind–body energy is essential – no question. But mind–body energy isn't the key for most chronic pain sufferers, especially when they feel so down, and when it can take months or years to master techniques such as meditation, guided imagery or self-hypnosis.

If all this talk about body–mind and mind–body sounds a bit mystical, please don't be put off by it. Love is a mystery, too, but it's as real as life itself. All we mean by body–mind energy is that when your body takes a successful step, your mind feels more hopeful. Likewise, when your mind feels more hopeful, your body tends to deal better with pain almost spontaneously. Given this kind of positive input, the body–mind/mind–body cycle keeps rotating, and as it does, the potential for recovery expands.

YOUR FIRST STEP TOWARD PHYSICAL RECOVERY

To take your first step toward physical recovery, all you need do is follow these simple steps:

1. Make a vow to yourself, here and now, to follow this plan's gradual approach to progress. Gradualism isn't a new or a complicated idea. But it is one of the few absolutely critical concepts in this book. In telephone calls that I made to 200 recovered chronic pain sufferers who provided input for this book, all rated gradualism as absolutely essential to restoring a shattered life to wellness. All 200 also said that it went *against* the very nature of what their lives had been like before being limited by chronic pain.

Why does taking things gradually go against the natural impulses of chronic pain sufferers? All of our lives, most of us take enormous pride in doing more and more. More is better; less is somehow shameful. If we have the flu and someone needs us, we drag ourselves out of bed and do whatever is necessary to help.

More is our mantra in this fast-paced world. More activities accomplished in the day. More tasks performed. More possessions owned. More speed. Less is not a word we like. Less money, less possessions, less of anything. Less doesn't work for us. We want to go fast. Speed matters. It matters with cars, reading, making dinner, shoveling snow, getting online and reaching personal goals. We want everything to go fast except the days of our lives. "Gradual pain relief" sounds absurd and unthinkable in comparison. Who would want that?

So, maybe it's time for a new mind-set. You simply must accept gradualism as a new way of thinking in order to get well as fast as possible. As a chronic pain sufferer, you have nothing in common with someone who is laid up with a sprained ankle, or a broken leg. The average person with a broken leg is up on crutches, hopping around, finding ways to perform super-human tasks as quickly as possible. And people applaud: "You sure are accomplishing a lot for someone with a broken leg."

As a chronic pain sufferer, you are more like the victim of a horrible accident. It's as if *all* of your limbs have been broken and *all* of your muscles and nerves have been bruised and altered in their functioning. It's as if you have been in chronic shock that has adversely affected your entire system – your mind, your body, your emotions, your faith, your spirit.

It's as if the self that you once knew and lived with has gone away and been replaced by a being that you hardly recognize or know. So many things you used to do routinely are now anything but routine. It isn't so much that you feel pain all of the time – which you do – it's more as if your life has been taken over by pain. Nothing has ever affected your life so profoundly and continuously.

Your new mantra, then, your new call to faith, is: gradual is faster. But what does this mean in practical terms for your daily life over the next month or two?

It means that you've got to change. *Your* needs are now your number one priority. It means that if a relative calls you and says, "Your cousin Tilly is getting married next week and you absolutely, positively have to be there as her matron of honor," you have to say, "Tell Tilly I'm terribly sorry, but I can't make it". It's hard but if you were deathly ill, and the doctor told you to stay in bed or risk dying, you would do it. But when you have chronic pain, it can feel feeble to say no. There are so many things you haven't been able to do. You've had to excuse yourself too many times. You fear that people will see you as a quitter.

The reality is people *might* think badly of you if you didn't attend a function in the first month or two of your recovery, because chronic pain isn't well understood in the way that herniated disks and pneumonia are. To the general public, chronic pain is something you should somehow be able to fight your way through. But now, in order to get well, you must proceed gradually and just forget about people's negative attitudes.

In a few moments, you'll choose a starting level of physical activity. And you'll see for yourself that everything about your recovery is riding on your belief in gradual progress. You *are* going to get to the finish line with maximum speed. You *are* going to recover. But you've got to give yourself a few months to reclaim the rest of your life. If you must make an exception because life just insists on it – you must attend a funeral, for example – please put this book away for two weeks, rest up and then come back to it.

2. Explain your recovery plan to family members or the people you're closest to. You want to gather as much understanding and support for your recovery as possible. Having family members or friends there for you, and backing your goals, isn't absolutely essential to your recovery, but it's a nice plus if you can get it.

If you've had chronic pain for a long time – the average survey participant for this book suffered incapacitating chronic pain for three and a half years before recovering – members of your family might be skeptical of any recovery plan. If this happens, you may find yourself having doubts. That's okay. Given what you've been through, you're entitled to have doubts.

So, how might you explain this book's recovery plan to a skeptic? I would put it this way: it works for chronic pain sufferers. There are no gimmicks. It's gradual and safe. And it takes just a few days to know whether or not it will work for you. Also, there is a built-in guarantee of success. You start off doing precisely the activities you are doing today, only 20 per cent less strenuously than you currently do. This guarantees you a successful outcome the first day. Within one week, depending on where you start the plan (see details later in this chapter), you'll be significantly more physically active than you are now. Within two weeks, you'll be doing more than you have in a long time.

To sum up, tell your family or friends that you're going to try a chronic pain recovery plan whose basic steps have succeeded for more than 1,000 people who had been everywhere and tried everything and despaired of ever getting well.

Now, an inevitable question: what if the plan *doesn't* work for you? Here's a straightforward answer: if you can be on your feet for at least five minutes at a time each day, and if you can walk at least one minute at a stretch each day, no matter how slowly or wobbly, and if your chronic pain problem is related to muscular difficulties that cannot be diagnosed as anything other than chronic pain, then this plan works. It works gradually, not overnight. It takes time. But it gets you there.

What if you can't make any progress? If that happens, it

won't be because you didn't try hard enough or because you had the wrong attitude. It would be for reasons that neither you nor I understand. But even in this highly unlikely scenario, all would not be lost, because you still have a guide to practitioners and treatments to help you find a way out of your chronic pain.

The final chapters of this book are devoted to rating practitioners and treatments for chronic pain: which professional treatments work, which don't work and which make people worse. It is important to read this section. Knowledge about chronic pain is your most powerful weapon, and your strongest defense against nonsensical and ineffectual treatments and procedures.

3. Arrange for a buddy to talk to you about your daily progress. Find yourself a "Plan Buddy", someone to chat with for two to three minutes a day about your progress. This buddy can be anyone at all – a family member, a colleague, a dear friend – but it must be someone kind, with an interest in you, and a good listener.

Reassure this person that two minutes a day is the most time you will need, and that you are not requiring so much support or encouragement as the benefit of talking out loud and validating your own daily progress.

For example, a "Plan Buddy" conversation might go something like this:

You: "I did well today. I was supposed to do one minute more walking, and one minute more activities around the house, and I did that. I'm feeling pretty good. In two weeks, if I maintain this gradual progress, I'll be walking __ minutes at a time and I'll be up and around __ minutes. One month from now, I will minimally have doubled my progress. In two months, I'll really have a life again."

Your Plan Buddy: "Sounds good. How do you feel?"

You: "I feel okay. Not entirely pain free. But the exercises that I'll be doing later on will help get me there. I'm starting to feel more up about things."

Your Plan Buddy: "You're making progress."

You: "Thanks for listening. I'll call you tomorrow."

This call took a total of about thirty seconds and in that time you've said to yourself, and to the world outside your pain, "I'm getting there." Just saying it, and having someone listen, helps. If you would rather not talk about your specific day-to-day progress, just say that you reached your goals for the day and you accomplished something. *Do* talk about where you'll be in two weeks or one month or two months, though. The seemingly small progress of any one day will feel better when you keep in mind the cumulative progress you can make over several weeks.

4. Vow to put fifteen minutes of relaxed enjoyment into each day. To put this in a more trendy way, you're going to do a mind–body activity for at least fifteen minutes every day. You're going to have some fun, some pure enjoyment, some time set aside for the sole purpose of doing something for yourself.

Is there scientific evidence that doing something fun will help your chronic pain? No, not the kind of evidence that would convince every scientist or skeptic, but having a good time every day can only help. Many survey participants in this book (60 per cent to be exact) felt that this kind of activity may well have helped them.

Which mind–body activity should you choose? Since you don't want to be slowed up at this point by the need to learn anything new – yoga or meditating, for example – rule out having to master a new skill. Also rule out anything that requires you to surmount a new physical challenge. Instead, rule in everything pleasurable and safe. Here are a few possibilities to inspire you:

- Anything you used to do, but gave up because you haven't felt mentally up for it. Knitting, for example. Or going to Lion's Club or Rotary Club meetings. Or doing volunteer work. Or spending time caring about dressing well and wearing make-up. Or just sitting on a bench in a park and enjoying people and nature.

- Reading a fast-paced novel, reading *The Bible*, reading magazines, reading about travel, reading about collecting stamps or coins, reading about food, nutrition, cooking, sports or anything else of personal interest to you.

- Praying. More survey participants advocated prayer than any other mind–body activity, and most of these individuals prayed both for the strength to get better as well as for the well-being of other people in their lives. If you believe in prayer, try speaking your prayers aloud, if privacy allows. Talk to God. Ask for the help that every human being needs in life.

- Listening, without distractions, to music that you love. Focus on the music and try to breathe it in and appreciate how much of life's joy and majesty it offers you.

- Watching comedy and other kinds of uplifting and inspiring videos. Laughing. Crying. Feeling the roar of life inside you and all about you.

- Talking to a friend. If it's appropriate, discuss your greatest fears and joys. Ask your friend about the greatest obstacles and challenges he or she has faced.

- Helping someone in need – either in person, online or through the mail. Really giving something of your inner self to someone. Reaching out. Being there for someone else.

- Singing. In the shower or out. As loud as you can or want to. Without a single thought about how well you do or don't sound. Sing along with a favourite singer or composer if you like, filling your lungs and belting it out. Fantasize that you're a great entertainer.

- Writing in a journal. We'll cover this mind-enriching activity in greater detail in chapter 12, "Mind–Body Healing." If you don't enjoy writing – if you're one of those people who shudders at the thought of facing a blank page – then skip this idea, at least for now. But if you do get pleasure out of expressing your feelings and your goals, and your daily progress, in writing, then . . . go for it! Every day, jot down a few of the thoughts going on inside your head about how you feel about your pain and yourself and your hopes for recovery. Plan a time to do this. Remember, you must want to do this, and get it done on a regular basis, for a minimum of fifteen minutes a day.

Think of your journal writings as confidential. Of course, if you want to share them, do so. But write for yourself – be serious, be funny, be brutally honest, be in writing who you are deep inside. I think you'll be delighted to find that, as you write, you'll get in touch with new truths about yourself.

- Hold a baby.
- Be with a loved one.

Feel free to choose more than one activity. For example, you might watch a comedy video (or part of one) one day, read a chapter of a great book the next day and pray for fifteen minutes the following day. Or you might pray every day and do one other activity that gives you something that's good for you. Feel free to indulge yourself and expand the requisite fifteen minutes of pleasure into several hours of having a wonderful time.

Remember, don't pick any activity that might frustrate you. Enjoy yourself. It may take a few days to get used to this pleasure you're receiving. Stay with it. Whatever effort you make, and whatever small or large pleasures you receive, will help you on the road to recovery.

5. Choose a starting level for walking (or swimming) and Stand-Up Daily Activities (SUDAS). Start by finding and ticking one category from the five below that best describes you. If you find yourself halfway between two categories, pick the easier one of the two. (Note: Category 1 is the most gentle and easy – for people who are mostly incapacitated. Category 5 is more challenging – for individuals who function fairly well, but still suffer ongoing discomfort.)

(Reminder: On Day 1, you're not going to be doing any more physical activity than you have been able to do even on your worst days. Nevertheless, if you have any feeling at all that being up and about

might be bad for you, consult with a healthcare practitioner before proceeding. In addition, as mentioned earlier, have a complete physical examination if you haven't already determined for certain that your chronic pain is not caused by an illness, tumor, blockage or any other disorder.)

CATEGORY 1: ALMOST ENTIRELY DISABLED

- Minimum ability to walk, without stopping, however slowly: five minutes. Maximum ability to walk without stopping: eight minutes.
- Minimum ability to be "up and about" without sitting: five minutes. Maximum ability to be "up and about" without sitting: ten minutes.

People in this category are usually bedridden or sedentary most of the time. Their pain prevents them from doing much of what they would like to do. They may be out of bed for an hour over the course of a day.

If you are not physically able to walk for five minutes at a stretch, but you can swim for at least three minutes at a stretch, proceed with this recovery plan, substituting swimming for walking. If you can only walk or swim, or only do the up-and-about activities, proceed with just that single activity. If you can neither walk, nor swim nor do up-and-about activities because you are in too much pain at this time, *do not proceed until your condition enables you to be out of bed, with no more than minor pain, for at least five minutes at a time.*

CATEGORY 2: MODERATELY DISABLED

- Minimum ability to walk, without stopping, at a gentle pace: nine minutes. Maximum ability to walk, without stopping: fourteen minutes.
- Minimum ability to be "up and about" without sitting: eleven minutes. Maximum ability to be "up and about" without sitting: thirty minutes.

People in this category cannot function normally during any given day, without paying a huge price for it. They aren't bedridden, but their condition is not a great deal better than that. Pain is often too severe to allow any sustained functioning. High-activity days are followed by several days of little or no activity.

If you are not physically able to walk for nine minutes at a stretch, but you can swim for five minutes at a stretch, or for five minutes with one break, proceed with this plan, substituting swimming for walking.

If you can only walk or swim, or only do the up-and-about activities, proceed with just that single category.

CATEGORY 3: SLIGHTLY DISABLED

- Minimum ability to walk, without stopping, at a gentle pace: fifteen minutes. Maximum ability to walk without stopping: thirty minutes.
- Minimum ability to be "up and about" without sitting: thirty minutes. Maximum ability to be "up and about" without sitting: sixty minutes.

People in this category often have part-time jobs and take breaks from time to time during their work hours. They rest after they get home. They do family activities and household tasks in spurts, resting in between.

If you are not physically able to walk for fifteen minutes at a stretch, but you can swim for eight minutes at a stretch, or for eight minutes with one or two breaks, proceed with this plan, substituting swimming for walking. If you can only walk or swim, or only do the up-and-about activities, proceed with just that single activity.

CATEGORY 4: OCCASIONALLY INCAPACITATED

- Minimum ability to walk without stopping: thirty minutes. Maximum ability to walk without stopping: sixty minutes.
- Minimum ability to be "up and about" without sitting: sixty minutes. Maximum ability to be "up and about" without sitting: seventy-five minutes.

People in this category tend to have a regular job, but with more frequent absences or down time than able-bodied people. They can function in spite of their misery, but must take enough breaks, usually lying down during the day, to avoid a relapse.

If you are not physically able to walk for thirty minutes at a stretch, but you can swim for twelve minutes at a stretch, or for twelve minutes with one, two or three breaks, proceed with this plan, substituting swimming for walking. If you can only walk or swim, or only do the up-and-about activities, proceed with just that single activity.

CATEGORY 5: FUNCTIONAL, BUT IN SOME PAIN MOST OR ALL OF THE TIME

- Minimum ability to walk without stopping: forty minutes. (There is no maximum ability for this category.)
- Minimum ability to be "up and about" without sitting: seventy-five minutes. (There is no maximum ability for this category.)

People in this category typically work at full-time jobs, but with some difficulty. They have bouts of pain that can put them on a lighter work schedule. For example, on a bad day, they might have to lie down to do their reading. Or they may have to stand, rather than sit, to do their paperwork. While driving on a trip, they may have to stop and stretch out or lie down in the back of the car from time to time. On a long plane trip, they may have to stand for part of the time. Sitting at a public event may be difficult for them.

If you are not physically able to walk for forty minutes at a stretch, but you can swim for fifteen minutes at a stretch, or for fifteen minutes with one, two or three breaks, proceed with this plan, substituting swimming for walking. If you can only walk or swim, or only do the up-and-about activities, proceed with that activity only.

Extra help in choosing a category

Did any questions occur to you when you read through the categories? Let's look at some different circumstances to make sure you know where to start and how to proceed.

Here are some questions about recovery that I was asked by chronic pain sufferers who were kind enough to read this manuscript before publication:

Q. You talk about people who walk regularly, or who can walk five minutes at a stretch. I've never measured the times of my walks, or "taken a walk". All told, though, I probably wind up walking thirty minutes every day if I include walking around the house, walking to the car, shopping and things like that. Which category should I choose?

A. If you don't walk on a regular or timed basis, forget the minimums/maximums for walking. Instead, select your category by how long you can be on your feet for any given period of time – what we call "up-and-about" time.

For example, let's say that on an average day, you can be on your feet for thirty minutes at a stretch. At this point, you have to sit down or lie down. However, on your worst days, you can be on your feet for an average of only fifteen minutes at a time. You belong in Category 2, where the minimum "up-and-about" time is eleven minutes and the maximum is thirty minutes.

Q. What do you mean by "worst days"? I have one or two catastrophic days every year and these are days when I stay in bed except to go to the bathroom. Then, every week or so, I have a bad day, where I have to cut down from four or five hours a day of functioning to about two hours.

A. Always go with your worst day to choose a starting category even if your worst days come just once or twice a year. This book has an underlying theme of "do no harm". If you can function only about two hours on your worst days, estimate how long you are up at any given time during those two hours. Let's say that number is forty-five minutes. You would choose Category 3.

Q. What if I'm just recovering from a terrible week, and I'm not doing anything normal at the moment?

A. Don't start this plan yet. Wait until you're back to some kind of norm. Then choose a starting category based on how you were at your absolute worst.

If you have any doubt about whether you should start this plan, don't start it.

If you have any doubt about which category to choose, choose Category 1 or 2. You want to eliminate all doubt about whether you can succeed on Day 1.

How to tackle Day 1 is coming up next, so . . . choose your category. Plan when you will walk or swim and when you will do your Stand-Up Activities. Good luck!

7

Day 1:
A Sixty-Second Checklist

Sixty seconds. Please read these words of encouragement before you start your first day's walk (or swim) and Stand-Up Daily Activities.

If you're like the average chronic pain sufferer, you've known more failure than success. You've heard more than your share of overblown promises of cures. You've tried hard to get well – without getting the results you want. Perhaps you've been to a famous doctor, or dozens of different doctors, or even experimented with a "miracle cure". Maybe you've tried a store shelf's worth of natural supplements, or taken a host of different prescription drugs.

This is all in the past now. Your past matters, but you can start your life anew at any instant in time. And that time is now.

Thirty-five seconds. The amount of walking (or swimming) that you're about to do is what you *know* you can do with relative ease. You've done it on your worst days. You have every reason to feel confident.

Taking a relatively short walk may seem like a baby step. It is, but as with baby steps, it leads to ongoing and life-changing growth and progress. Within two weeks, there is every realistic chance that you'll be doing better than you've done in a long time, no matter how incapacitated you may be.

Twenty seconds. Relax. Move your neck slowly from side to side. Shrug your shoulders gently. Take a deep breath from your belly and exhale slowly through your mouth.

The big challenge was to read this far. To accept the difficult times you've been through and to move on. You have the love and admiration of a world of chronic pain sufferers. What comes next is relatively easy.

Hold this final thought: if you don't believe in yourself, that's okay. Just take the next step.

8

Days 2–14 and Beyond

Congratulations! You've taken your first day's walk (or swim) and performed your first day's Stand-Up Daily Activities (SUDAS). Each day will now bring you measurably closer to your goal of recovery and wellness.

Right now, before you start Day 2, take a piece of paper and a pen – or work at a computer – to create a simple Recovery Progress Chart. Just follow the steps below. (To make sure that you set up your Recovery Progress Chart correctly – and to have a quick summary of what you'll need to know to carry out your plan – please look at the sample charts for each category at the end of this chapter.)

1. Put a title on the top of the page: "Recovery Progress Chart for [fill in your name]." Print neatly or type. Make your sheet of paper look official. In two weeks, this important document is going to become a log of the substantial progress you've made. In a month or two, it will be a detailed record of how you turned around chronic pain and found a new life for yourself.
2. Write or type in headings like those you see in the chart on the next page.

Fill in what you did on Day 1: how many minutes you actually walked, or swam, and did Stand-Up Daily Activities. (The chart below gives made-up numbers for an imaginary Jane Doe.)

Recovery Chart for Jane Doe

Day 1	Walking (minutes)	SUDAS (minutes)
Monday, August 1	6	6

Write in the actual dates for Days 2–14. Make sure that Day 2 is today's date and that the activity times are yours, not the imaginary Jane Doe's. At the end of each day, fill in your times. Your chart will now look like this, except that the dates and numbers will be your own.

Recovery Chart for Jane Doe

Day	Walking (minutes)	SUDAS (minutes)
1 – Monday, August 5	12	18
2 – Tuesday, August 6		
3 – Wednesday, August 7		
4 – Thursday, August 8		
5 – Friday, August 9		
6 – Saturday, August 10		
7 – Sunday, August 11		
8 – Monday, August 12		
9 – Tuesday, August 13		
10 – Wednesday, August 14		
11 – Thursday, August 15		
12 – Friday, August 16		
13 – Saturday, August 17		
14 – Sunday, August 18		

How much progress will you make in two weeks? In two months?

In just two weeks, you will be at least 33 per cent better than you've been in a long time. And, you will have established a solid base from which to move ahead with ever-faster speed to an active life.

Here are five examples of the progress a chronic pain sufferer can make using this book's Body–Mind Recovery Plan. To get a good idea of how well *you* can do, just look at the category that you have assigned yourself.

CATEGORY 1: ALMOST ENTIRELY DISABLED

In this example, Jane Doe could walk only five minutes a day on her worst days, so she started Day 1 at 20 per cent less than five minutes – or, four minutes. This means that she started at just four minutes of walking on Day 1. Similarly, she started at just four minutes of SUDAS.

Each day for the first week, Jane increased her progress by thirty seconds. Each day for the second week, Jane increased her progress by one minute. Here is Jane's progress for two weeks:

Recovery Chart for Jane Doe, Days 1–14		
Day	*Walking* *(minutes)*	*SUDAS* *(minutes)*
1 – Monday, August 5	4	4
2 – Tuesday, August 6	4½	4½
3 – Wednesday, August 7	5	5
4 – Thursday, August 8	5½	5½
5 – Friday, August 9	6	6
6 Saturday, August 10	6½	6½
7 – Sunday, August 11	7	7
[For Week 2, in this example, Jane Doe now advances by one minute each day]		
8 – Monday, August 12	8	8
9 – Tuesday, August 13	9	9
10 – Wednesday, August 14	10	10
11 – Thursday, August 15	11	11
12 – Friday, August 16	12	12
13 – Saturday, August 17	13	13
14 – Sunday, August 18	14	14

SUMMARY OF PROGRESS IN TWO WEEKS FOR CATEGORY 1: *Almost triple the amount of walking, Stand-Up Daily Activities (SUDAS) and overall time being active.*

If Jane chooses to swim, instead of walk – and if she paces her time increases as shown in the next chart – her recovery will proceed as follows:

A look at progress with swimming instead of walking

Recovery Chart for Jane Doe, Days 1–14		
Day	Walking (minutes)	SUDAS (minutes)
1 – Monday, August 5	3	4
2 – Tuesday, August 6	3	4½
3 – Wednesday, August 7	3½	5
4 – Thursday, August 8	3½	5½
5 – Friday, August 9	4	6
6 – Saturday, August 10	4	6½
7 – Sunday, August 11	4½	7
8 – Monday, August 12	4½	8
9 – Tuesday, August 13	5	9
10 – Wednesday, August 14	5	10
11 – Thursday, August 15	5½	11
12 – Friday, August 16	5½	12
13 – Saturday, August 17	6	13
14 – Sunday, August 18	6	14

SUMMARY OF PROGRESS IN TWO WEEKS FOR CATEGORY 1: *Double the amount of swimming. More than triple the amount of Stand-Up Daily Activities (SUDAS).*

Where will this once almost entirely disabled person be in six weeks? In twelve weeks?

Jane will advance two minutes a day, Day 15–Day 21. She will advance three minutes a day, Day 22–Day 28. At the end of Day 28, she will be walking her Maximum Daily Walk of forty-five minutes. She will be doing SUDAS for forty-nine minutes a day. For Days 29–42 Jane will consolidate her gains and continue to advance at the rate of three minutes each day. She will also start her stretching/strengthening exercise programmeme during this time. At the end of this six-week period, she will be doing Stand-Up Daily Activities for about an hour and a half at a stretch. Her total Minimum Up Time will be about two and a quarter hours a day, including walking time.

For Days 43–49 and 50–56, Jane will increase her daily SUDAS by four minutes each day. In each successive seven-day period, she will increase her advances by one more minute per day. At the end of twelve weeks (84 days – less than three full months from the day that she started as a near-invalid) Jane will be taking a Maximum Daily Walk of forty-five minutes and she will be doing SUDAS five and one-half hours a day. Her total Minimum Up Time will be about six hours. With a few carefully planned, uninterrupted rest breaks, Jane will now manage to work a substantial work day.

Here's a summary of Jane's progress, Week 3–Week 12:

Recovery Chart for Jane Doe, Week 3–Week 12		
Week	Walking per day by the end of the week (minutes)	SUDAS per day by the end of the week (minutes)
3 (Days 15–21)	28	28
4 (Days 22–28)	45 (Maximum Daily Walk)	49
5 (Days 29–35)	45	70
6 (Days 36–42)	45	119
7 (Days 43–49)	45	147
8 (Days 50–56)	45	182
9 (Days 57–63)	45	224
10 (Days 64–70)	45	273
11 (Days 71–77)	45	329
12 (Days 78–84)	45	392
		(about $6\frac{1}{2}$ hrs)

If Jane swims, and paces her time increases as shown in the next chart, her recovery will proceed as follows:

Progress with swimming instead of walking

Recovery Chart for Jane Doe, Week 3–Week 12		
Week	Swimming per day by the end of the week (minutes)	SUDAS per day by the end of the week (minutes)
3 (Days 15–21)	7	28
4 (Days 22–28)	8	49
5 (Days 29–35)	9	70
6 (Days 36–42)	10	91
7 (Days 43–49)	11	119
8 (Days 50–56)	12	147
9 (Days 57–63)	14	182
10 (Days 64–70)	16	224
11 (Days 71–77)	18	273
12 (Days 78–84)	20	329 (5½ hrs)

CATEGORY 2: MODERATELY DISABLED

In this example, John Doe can walk only fifteen minutes a day on his worst days, so he starts Day 1 at 20 per cent less than fifteen minutes – or twelve minutes. That means he walks twelve consecutive minutes on Day 1. He starts SUDAS at 20 per cent below his worst-day number of thirty-four minutes.

Each day for the first week, John increases his progress by one minute. Each day for the second week, John increases his progress by ninety seconds. Here is John's progress over two weeks:

Recovery Chart for John Doe, Days 1–14		
Day	Walking (minutes)	SUDAS (minutes)
1 – Monday, August 5	12	27
2 – Tuesday, August 6	13	28
3 – Wednesday, August 7	14	29

4 – Thursday, August 8	15	30
5 – Friday, August 9	16	31
6 – Saturday, August 10	17	32
7 – Sunday, August 11	18	33

[In this example, John Doe now advances
by 90 seconds each day]

8 – Monday, August 12	$19\frac{1}{2}$	$34\frac{1}{2}$
9 – Tuesday, August 13	21	36
10 – Wednesday, August 14	$22\frac{1}{2}$	$37\frac{1}{2}$
11 – Thursday, August 15	24	39
12 – Friday, August 16	$25\frac{1}{2}$	$40\frac{1}{2}$
13 – Saturday, August 17	27	42
14 – Sunday, August 18	$28\frac{1}{2}$	$43\frac{1}{2}$

SUMMARY OF PROGRESS IN TWO WEEKS FOR CATEGORY 2: *About $2\frac{1}{2}$ times as much walking. More than twice the Minimum Daily Up Time (minimum time walking, standing or sitting during the day).*

If John chooses to swim, instead of walk – and if he paces his time increases as shown in the next chart – his recovery will proceed as follows:

Progress with swimming instead of walking

Recovery Chart for John Doe, Days 1–14		
Day	*Swimming (minutes)*	*SUDAS (minutes)*
1 – Monday, August 5	4	27
2 – Tuesday, August 6	$4\frac{1}{2}$	28
3 – Wednesday, August 7	5	29
4 – Thursday, August 8	$5\frac{1}{2}$	30
5 – Friday, August 9	6	31
6 – Saturday, August 10	$6\frac{1}{2}$	32
7 – Sunday, August 11	7	33

8 – Monday, August 12	7½	34½
9 – Tuesday, August 13	8	36
10 – Wednesday, August 14	8½	37½
11 – Thursday, August 15	9	39
12 – Friday, August 16	9½	40½
13 – Saturday, August 17	10	42
14 – Sunday, August 18	10½	43½

SUMMARY OF PROGRESS IN TWO WEEKS FOR CATEGORY 2: *About 2½ times as much swimming. Nearly twice the Minimum Daily Up Time (minimum time walking, standing or sitting during the day).*

Where will this once moderately disabled person be in six weeks? In twelve weeks?

John will advance two minutes a day, Day 15–Day 21. He will advance three minutes a day, Day 22–Day 28. At the end of Day 28, he will be walking a Maximum Daily Walk of forty-five minutes. He will be doing SUDAS for forty-nine minutes a day.

For Days 29–35, John will consolidate his gains and continue to advance at the rate of three minutes each day. For Days 36–42, John will increase his rate of progress by four minutes each day. He also will start his stretching/strengthening exercise programme during this time. At the end of this six-week period, he will be doing Stand-Up Daily Activities for about two hours at a stretch. His total Minimum Up Time will be nearly three hours a day, including walking time.

Starting with days 43–49 (Week 7), John will increase his daily SUDAS by one additional minute each day. At the end of twelve weeks (eighty-four days) – less than three full months from the day he started as a moderately incapacitated chronic pain sufferer – John will be taking a Maximum Daily Walk of fifty-four minutes and he will be doing SUDAS nearly seven and a half hours a day. His total Minimum Up Time will be more than eight and a quarter hours. Include a few rest breaks and John will now be able to work a full work day.

Here's a summary of John's progress, Week 3–Week 12:

Recovery Chart for John Doe, Week 3–Week 12		
Week	Walking per day by the end of the week (minutes	SUDAS per day by the end of the week (minutes)
3 (Days 15–21)	About 42	About 57
4 (Days 22–28)	45 (Maximum Daily Walk)	78
5 (Days 29–35)	45	99
6 (Days 36—42)	45	127
7 (Days 43–49)	45	162
8 (Days 50–56)	45	204
9 (Days 57–63)	45	253
10 (Days 64–70)	45	309
11 (Days 71–77)	45	372
12 (Days 78–84)	45	442 (nearly $7^1/_2$ hrs)

If John swims, and paces his time increases as shown in the next chart, his recovery will proceed as follows:

Progress with swimming instead of walking

Recovery Chart for John Doe, Week 3–Week 12		
Week	Swimming per day by the end of the week (minutes)	SUDAS per day by the end of the week (minutes)
3 (Days 15-21)	14	About 57
4 (Days 22-28)	14	78
5 (Days 29-35)	14	99
6 (Days 36-42)	$17^1/_2$	127
7 (Days 43-49)	$17^1/_2$	162
8 (Days 50-56)	$17^1/_2$	204
9 (Days 57-63)	21	253
10 (Days 64-70)	21	309
11 (Days 71-77)	21	372
12 (Days 78-84)	21	442 (nearly $7^1/_2$ hrs)

CATEGORY 3: SLIGHTLY DISABLED

In this example, Mary Smith can walk twenty consecutive minutes a day on her worst days, so she starts Day 1 at 20 per cent less than twenty minutes – or sixteen minutes. Mary walks sixteen consecutive minutes on Day 1. She starts SUDAS at forty minutes, 20 per cent below her worst-day number of fifty minutes.

Each day for the first week, Mary increases her progress by one minute. Each day for the second week, Mary increases her progress by two minutes. Here is Mary's progress over two weeks:

Recovery Chart for Mary Smith, Days 1–14		
Day	Walking (minutes)	SUDAS (minutes)
1 – Monday, August 5	16	40
2 – Tuesday, August 6	17	41
3 – Wednesday, August 7	18	42
4 – Thursday, August 8	19	43
5 – Friday, August 9	20	44
6 – Saturday, August 10	21	45
7 – Sunday, August 11	22	46
[In this example, Mary Doe now advances by two minutes each day]		
8 – Monday, August 12	24	48
9 – Tuesday, August 13	26	50
10 – Wednesday, August 14	28	52
11 – Thursday, August 15	30	54
12 – Friday, August 16	32	56
13 – Saturday, August 17	34	58
14 – Sunday, August 18	36	60

SUMMARY OF PROGRESS IN TWO WEEKS FOR CATEGORY 3: *Nearly twice as much walking and almost twice as much Minimum Daily Up Time (minimum time walking, standing or sitting during the day).*

If Mary chooses to swim, instead of walk – and if she paces her time increases as shown in the next chart – her recovery will proceed as follows:

Progress with swimming instead of walking

Recovery Chart for Mary Smith, Days 1–14		
Day	Swimming per day by end of the week (minutes)	SUDAS per day by end of the week (minutes)
1 – Monday, August 5	6	40
2 – Tuesday, August 6	7	41
3 – Wednesday, August 7	8	42
4 – Thursday, August 8	9	43
5 – Friday, August 9	10	44
6 – Saturday, August 10	11	45
7 – Sunday, August 11	12	46
8 – Monday, August 12	13	48
9 – Tuesday, August 13	14	50
10 – Wednesday, August 14	15	52
11 – Thursday, August 15	16	54
12 – Friday, August 16	17	56
13 – Saturday, August 17	18	58
14 – Sunday, August 18	19	60

SUMMARY OF PROGRESS IN TWO WEEKS FOR CATEGORY 3: *Three times as much swimming and 50% more Minimum Daily Up Time (minimum time walking, standing or sitting during the day).*

Where will this once slightly disabled person be in six weeks? In twelve weeks?

Mary will advance three minutes a day, Day 15–Day 21 and also start her stretching/strengthening exercise programme during this time. She will advance four minutes a day, Day

22–Day 28 and Day 29–35. She will advance five minutes a day, Day 36–42.

At the end of this six-week period, Mary will be doing Stand-Up Daily Activities for nearly three hours at a stretch. Her total Minimum Up Time will be nearly four hours, including walking time.

Starting with Days 43–49 (Week 7) Mary will increase her daily SUDAS by one additional minute each day. At the end of twelve weeks (eighty-four days) – less than three full months from the day she started as a slightly incapacitated chronic pain sufferer – Mary will be taking a Maximum Daily Walk of sixty minutes and, additionally, she will be doing SUDAS almost nine hours a day. With a short break after work, she will be able to enjoy a full day and evening.

Here's a summary of Mary's progress, Week 3–Week 12:

Recovery Chart for Mary Smith, Week 3–Week 12

Week	Walking per day by the end of the week (minutes)	SUDAS per day by the end of the week (minutes)
3 (Days 15–21)	57	81
4 (Days 22–28)	60 (Maximum Daily Walk)	109
5 (Days 29–35)	60	137
6 (Days 36–42)	60	172
7 (Days 43–49)	60	214
8 (Days 50–56)	60	263
9 (Days 57–63)	60	319
10 (Days 64–70)	60	382
11 (Days 71–77)	60	452
12 (Days 78–84)	60	529 (almost 9 hrs)

If Mary swims, and paces her time increases as shown in the next chart, her recovery will proceed as follows:

Progress with swimming instead of walking

Recovery Chart for Mary Smith, Week 3–Week 12		
Week	Swimming per day by the end of the week (minutes)	SUDAS per day by the end of the week (minutes)
3 (Days 15–21)	22½	81
4 (Days 22–28)	22½	109
5 (Days 29–35)	26	137
6 (Days 36–42)	26	172
7 (Days 43–49)	26	214
8 (Days 50–56)	30 (maximum)	263
9 (Days 57–63)	30	319
10 (Days 64–70)	30	382
11 (Days 71–77)	30	452
12 (Days 78–84)	30	529 (almost 9 hrs)

CATEGORY 4: OCCASIONALLY INCAPACITATED

In this example, Mark Smith can walk forty consecutive minutes a day on his worst days, so he starts Day 1 at 20 per cent less than forty minutes – or thirty-two minutes. Mark walks thirty-two consecutive minutes on Day 1. He starts SUDAS at seventy-two minutes, 20 per cent below his worst-day number of ninety minutes.

Each day for the first week, Mark increases his progress by two minutes. Each day for the second week, Mark increases his progress by three minutes. Here is Mark's progress over two weeks:

Recovery Chart for Mark Smith, Days 1–14

Day	Walking (minutes)	SUDAS (minutes)
1 – Monday, August 5	32	72
2 – Tuesday, August 6	34	74
3 – Wednesday, August 7	36	76
4 – Thursday, August 8	38	78
5 – Friday, August 9	40	80
6 – Saturday, August 10	42	82
7 – Sunday, August 11	44	84
[In this example, Mark Smith now advances by three minutes each day]		
8 – Monday, August 12	47	87
9 – Tuesday, August 13	50	90
10 – Wednesday, August 14	53	91
11 – Thursday, August 15	56	94
12 – Friday, August 16	59	97
13 – Saturday, August 17	60 (maximum)	100
14 – Sunday, August 18	60	103

SUMMARY OF PROGRESS IN TWO WEEKS FOR CATEGORY 3: *Nearly twice as much walking. About 60% more Minimum Daily Up Time (minimum time walking, standing or sitting during the day).*

If Mark chooses to swim, instead of walk – and if he paces his time increases as shown in the next chart – his recovery will proceed as follows:

Progress with swimming instead of walking

Recovery Chart for Mark Smith, Days 1–14

Day	Swimming (minutes)	SUDAS (minutes)
1 – Monday, August 5	12	72
2 – Tuesday, August 6	13	74

3 – Wednesday, August 7	14	76
4 – Thursday, August 8	15	78
5 – Friday, August 9	16	80
6 – Saturday, August 10	17	82
7 – Sunday, August 11	18	84
8 – Monday, August 12	19	87
9 – Tuesday, August 13	20	90
10 – Wednesday, August 14	21	91
11 – Thursday, August 15	22	94
12 – Friday, August 16	23	97
13 – Saturday, August 17	24	100
14 – Sunday, August 18	25	103

SUMMARY OF PROGRESS IN TWO WEEKS FOR CATEGORY 3: *Twice as much swimming. Nearly 50% more Minimum Daily Up Time (minimum time walking, standing or sitting during the day).*

Where will this once occasionally disabled person be in six weeks? In twelve weeks?

Mark will advance four minutes a day, Day 15–Day 21 and also start his stretching/strengthening exercise programme during this time. He will advance five minutes a day, Day 22–Day 28 . . . six minutes a day, Days 29–35 . . . and seven minutes a day, Days 36–42.

At the end of this six-week period, Mark will be doing Stand-Up Daily Activities for more than four hours at a stretch. His total Minimum Up Time will be about five and a quarter hours a day, including walking time.

Starting with Days 43–49 (Week 7) Mark will increase his daily SUDAS by one additional minute each day. At the end of twelve weeks (eighty-four days) – less than three full months from the day he started as a slightly incapacitated chronic pain sufferer – Mark will be taking a Maximum Daily Walk of sixty minutes and, additionally, he will be doing SUDAS more than eleven hours a day. With an occasional short break, he will be able to enjoy a full day and evening.

Here's a summary of Mark's progress, Week 3–Week 12:

Recovery Chart for Mark Smith, Week 3–Week 12		
Week	Walking per day by the end of the week (minutes)	SUDAS per day by the end of the week (minutes)
3 (Days 15–21)	60 (Maximum Daily Walk)	131
4 (Days 22-28)	60	166
5 (Days 29-35)	60	208
6 (Days 36-42)	60	257
7 (Days 43-49)	60	313
8 (Days 50-56)	60	376
9 (Days 57-63)	60	446
10 (Days 64-70)	60	523
11 (Days 71-77)	60	607
12 (Days 78-84)	60	698
		(more than $11\frac{1}{2}$ hrs)

If Mark swims, and paces his time increases as shown in the next chart, his recovery will proceed as follows:

Progress with swimming instead of walking

Recovery Chart for Mark Smith, Week 3–Week 12		
Week	Swimming per day by the end of the week (minutes)	SUDAS per day by the end of the week (minutes)
3 (Days 15–21)	$28\frac{1}{2}$	131
4 (Days 22–28)	32	166
5 (Days 29–35)	35 (maximum)	208
6 (Days 36–42)	35	257
7 (Days 43–49)	35	313
8 (Days 50–56)	35	376
9 (Days 57–63)	35	446
10 (Days 64–70)	35	523
11 (Days 71–77)	35	607
12 (Days 78–84)	35	698
		(more than $11\frac{1}{2}$ hrs)

CATEGORY 5: FUNCTIONAL BUT IN SOME PAIN MOST OF THE TIME

In this example, Patricia Jones can walk forty-five consecutive minutes a day on her worst days, so she starts Day 1 at 20 per cent less than forty-five minutes – or, thirty-six minutes. Patricia walks thirty-six consecutive minutes on Day 1. She starts SUDAS at 120 minutes, 20 per cent below her worst-day number of two and a half hours (150 minutes).

Each day for the first week, Patricia increases her progress by three minutes. Each day for the second week, Patricia increases her progress by five minutes. Here is Patricia's progress over two weeks:

Recovery Chart for Patricia Jones, Days 1–14		
Day	*Walking (minutes)*	*SUDAS (minutes)*
1 – Monday, August 5	36	150
2 – Tuesday, August 6	39	153
3 – Wednesday, August 7	42	156
4 – Thursday, August 8	45	159
5 – Friday, August 9	48	162
6 – Saturday, August 10	51	165
7 – Sunday, August 11	54	168
[In this example, Patricia Jones now advances by five minutes each day]		
8 – Monday, August 12	59	173
9 – Tuesday, August 13	60 (Maximum) Daily Walk)	178
10 – Wednesday, August 14	60	183
11 – Thursday, August 15	60	188
12 – Friday, August 16	60	193
13 – Saturday, August 17	60	198
14 – Sunday, August 18	60	203

SUMMARY OF PROGRESS IN TWO WEEKS FOR CATEGORY 5: *Some 70% more walking. About 50% more Minimum Daily Up Time (minimum time walking, standing or sitting during the day).*

If Patricia chooses to swim, instead of walk – and if she paces her time increases as shown in the next chart – her recovery will proceed as follows:

Progress with swimming instead of walking

Recovery Chart for Patricia Jones, Days 1–14

Day	Swimming (minutes)	SUDAS (minutes)
1 – Monday, August 5	12	150
2 – Tuesday, August 6	13	153
3 – Wednesday, August 7	14	156
4 – Thursday, August 8	15	159
5 – Friday, August 9	16	162
6 – Saturday, August 10	17	165
7 – Sunday, August 11	18	168
8 – Monday, August 12	19	173
9 – Tuesday, August 13	20	178
10 – Wednesday, August 14	21	183
11 – Thursday, August 15	22	188
12 – Friday, August 16	23	193
13 – Saturday, August 17	24	198
14 – Sunday, August 18	25	203

SUMMARY OF PROGRESS IN TWO WEEKS FOR CATEGORY 5: *Twice as much swimming. Nearly 50% more Minimum Daily Up Time (minimum time walking, standing or sitting during the day).*

Where will this functional chronic pain sufferer be in six weeks? In eight weeks?

Patricia will advance seven minutes a day, Day 15–Day 21 and also start her stretching/strengthening exercise programme during this time. She will advance nine minutes a day, Day 22–Day 28 . . . 11 minutes a day, Day 29–35 . . . and thirteen minutes a day, Day 36–42.

At the end of this six-week period, Patricia will be doing Stand-Up Daily Activities for more than eight hours at a stretch. Her total Minimum Up Time will be nine hours a day, including walking time.

Starting with Day 43–49 (Week 7) Patricia will increase her daily SUDAS by two additional minutes each day. At the end of eight weeks (56 days), Patricia will be taking a Maximum Daily Walk of sixty minutes and, additionally, she will be doing SUDAS nearly twelve hours a day. With an occasional break as needed, she will be able to enjoy a full day and evening with a minimum of pain.

Here's a summary of Patricia's progress, Week 3–Week 8:

Recovery Chart for Patricia Jones, Week 3–Week 8		
Week	Walking per day by the end of the week (minutes)	SUDAS per day by the end of the week (minutes)
3 (Days 15–21)	60 (Maximum Daily Walk)	252
4 (Days 22–28)	60	315
5 (Days 29–35)	60	392
6 (Days 36–42)	60	483
7 (Days 43–49)	60	588
8 (Days 50–56)	60	707 (nearly 12 hrs)

If Patricia swims, and paces her time increases as shown in the next chart, her recovery will proceed as follows:

Progress with swimming instead of walking

Recovery Chart for Patricia Jones, Week 3–Week 8		
Week	Swimming per day by the end of the week (minutes)	SUDAS per day by the end of the week (minutes)
3 (Days 15–21)	28½	252
4 (Days 22–28)	32	315
5 (Days 29–35)	35½	392
6 (Days 36–42)	40 (maximum)	483
7 (Days 43–49)	40	588
8 (Days 50–56)	40	707
		(nearly 12 hrs)

SUMMARY

You've started to make success a routine part of your day – congratulations! Remember to keep up with your fifteen minutes of daily enjoyment, your special buddy, and your chart.

You are well on your way to a great triumph over months, years or decades of adversity – and also well on your way to the life you want.

The following pages provide summaries of each Body–Mind Recovery Plan, Categories 1–5.

Category 1: Almost entirely disabled
Recovery Progress Report for

_____

	Date	Walking	(Or . . . Swimming)	SUDAS
WEEK 1		Add 30 seconds per day	Add 30 seconds every other day	Add 30 seconds per day
Day 1	_____	_____	_____	_____
Day 2	_____	_____	_____	_____
Day 3	_____	_____	_____	_____
Day 4	_____	_____	_____	_____
Day 5	_____	_____	_____	_____
Day 6	_____	_____	_____	_____
Day 7	_____	_____	_____	_____
WEEK 2		Add 1 minute per day	Add 30 seconds every other day	Add 1 minute per day
Day 8	_____	_____	_____	_____
Day 9	_____	_____	_____	_____
Day 10	_____	_____	_____	_____
Day 11	_____	_____		_____
Day 12	_____	_____	_____	_____
Day 13	_____	_____	_____	_____
Day 14	_____	_____	_____	_____

	Date	Walking	(Or ... Swimming)	SUDAS
WEEK 3		Add 2 minutes per day	Add 30 seconds twice a week	Add 2 minutes per day
Day 15	_____	_____	_____	_____
Day 16	_____	_____	_____	_____
Day 17	_____	_____	_____	_____
Day 18	_____	_____	_____	_____
Day 19	_____	_____	_____	_____
Day 20	_____	_____	_____	_____
Day 21	_____	_____	_____	_____
WEEK 4		Add 3 minutes per day	Add 30 seconds twice a week	Add 3 minutes per day
Day 22	_____	_____	_____	_____
Day 23	_____	_____	_____	_____
Day 24	_____	_____	_____	_____
Day 25	_____	_____	_____	_____
Day 26	_____	_____	_____	_____
Day 27	_____	_____	_____	_____
Day 28	_____	_____	_____	_____
WEEK 5		45-minute walk	Add 30 seconds twice a week	Add 3 minutes per day
Day 29	_____	_____	_____	_____
Day 30	_____	_____	_____	_____
Day 31	_____	_____	_____	_____
Day 32	_____	_____	_____	_____
Day 33	_____	_____	_____	_____
Day 34	_____	_____	_____	_____
Day 35	_____	_____	_____	_____

	Date	Walking	(Or . . . Swimming)	SUDAS
WEEK 6		45-minute walk	Add 30 seconds twice a week	Add 3 minutes per day
Day 36	_____	_____	_____	_____
Day 37	_____	_____	_____	_____
Day 38	_____	_____	_____	_____
Day 39	_____	_____	_____	_____
Day 40	_____	_____	_____	_____
Day 41	_____	_____	_____	_____
Day 42	_____	_____	_____	_____
WEEK 7		45-minute walk	Add 30 seconds twice a week	Add 4 minutes per day
Day 43	_____	_____	_____	_____
Day 44	_____	_____	_____	_____
Day 45	_____	_____	_____	_____
Day 46	_____	_____	_____	_____
Day 47	_____	_____	_____	_____
Day 48	_____	_____	_____	_____
Day 49	_____	_____	_____	_____
WEEK 8		45-minute walk	Add 30 seconds twice a week	Add 4 minutes per day
Day 50	_____	_____	_____	_____
Day 51	_____	_____	_____	_____
Day 52	_____	_____	_____	_____
Day 53	_____	_____	_____	_____
Day 54	_____	_____	_____	_____
Day 55	_____	_____	_____	_____
Day 56	_____	_____	_____	_____

Date	Walking	(Or . . . Swimming)	SUDAS
WEEK 9	45-minute walk	Add 30 seconds twice a week	Add 5 minutes per day
Day 57 _____	_____	_____	_____
Day 58 _____	_____	_____	_____
Day 59 _____	_____	_____	_____
Day 60 _____	_____	_____	_____
Day 61 _____	_____	_____	_____
Day 62 _____	_____	_____	_____
Day 63 _____	_____	_____	_____
WEEK 10	45-minute walk	Add 30 seconds twice a week	Add 6 minutes per day
Day 64 _____	_____	_____	_____
Day 65 _____	_____	_____	_____
Day 66 _____	_____	_____	_____
Day 67 _____	_____	_____	_____
Day 68 _____	_____	_____	_____
Day 69 _____	_____	_____	_____
Day 70 _____	_____	_____	_____
WEEK 11	45-minute walk	Add 30 seconds twice a week	Add 7 minutes per day
Day 71 _____	_____	_____	_____
Day 72 _____	_____	_____	_____
Day 73 _____	_____	_____	_____
Day 74 _____	_____	_____	_____
Day 75 _____	_____	_____	_____
Day 76 _____	_____	_____	_____
Day 77 _____	_____	_____	_____

	Date	Walking	(Or . . . Swimming)	SUDAS
WEEK 12		45-minute walk	Add 30 seconds twice a week	Add 8 minutes per day
Day 78	_____	_____	_____	_____
Day 79	_____	_____	_____	_____
Day 80	_____	_____	_____	_____
Day 81	_____	_____	_____	_____
Day 82	_____	_____	_____	_____
Day 83	_____	_____	_____	_____
Day 84	_____	_____	_____	_____

Category 2: Moderately disabled
Recovery Progress Report for

_____

	Date	Walking	(Or ... Swimming)	SUDAS
WEEK 1		Add 1 minute per day	Add 30 seconds every day	Add 1 minute per day
Day 1	____	____	____	____
Day 2	____	____	____	____
Day 3	____	____	____	____
Day 4	____	____	____	____
Day 5	____	____	____	____
Day 6	____	____	____	____
Day 7	____	____	____	____
WEEK 2		Add $1\frac{1}{2}$ minutes per day	Add 30 seconds every day	Add $1\frac{1}{2}$ minutes per day
Day 8	____	____	____	____
Day 9	____	____	____	____
Day 10	____	____	____	____
Day 11	____	____	____	____
Day 12	____	____	____	____
Day 13	____	____	____	____
Day 14	____	____	____	____

	Date	Walking	(Or . . . Swimming)	SUDAS
WEEK 3		Add 2 minutes per day (Max. walk: 45 min.)	Add 30 seconds twice a week	Add 2 minutes per day
Day 15	_____	_____	_____	_____
Day 16	_____	_____	_____	_____
Day 17	_____	_____	_____	_____
Day 18	_____	_____	_____	_____
Day 19	_____	_____	_____	_____
Day 20	_____	_____	_____	_____
Day 21	_____	_____	_____	_____
WEEK 4		45-minute walk	Maintain time	Add 3 minutes per day
Day 22	_____	_____	_____	_____
Day 23	_____	_____	_____	_____
Day 24	_____	_____	_____	_____
Day 25	_____	_____	_____	_____
Day 26	_____	_____	_____	_____
Day 27	_____	_____	_____	_____
Day 28	_____	_____	_____	_____
WEEK 5		45-minute walk	Maintain time	Add 3 minutes per day
Day 29	_____	_____	_____	_____
Day 30	_____	_____	_____	_____
Day 31	_____	_____	_____	_____
Day 32	_____	_____	_____	_____
Day 33	_____	_____	_____	_____
Day 34	_____	_____	_____	_____
Day 35	_____	_____	_____	_____

	Date	Walking	(Or . . . Swimming)	SUDAS
WEEK 6		45-minute walk	Add 30 seconds every day	Add 4 minutes per day
Day 36	_____	_____	_____	_____
Day 37	_____	_____	_____	_____
Day 38	_____	_____	_____	_____
Day 39	_____	_____	_____	_____
Day 40	_____	_____	_____	_____
Day 41	_____	_____	_____	_____
Day 42	_____	_____	_____	_____
WEEK 7		45-minute walk	Maintain	Add 5 minutes per day
Day 43	_____	_____	_____	_____
Day 44	_____	_____	_____	_____
Day 45	_____	_____	_____	_____
Day 46	_____	_____	_____	_____
Day 47	_____	_____	_____	_____
Day 48	_____	_____	_____	_____
Day 49	_____	_____	_____	_____
WEEK 8		45-minute walk	Maintain	Add 6 minutes per day
Day 50	_____	_____	_____	_____
Day 51	_____	_____	_____	_____
Day 52	_____	_____	_____	_____
Day 53	_____	_____	_____	_____
Day 54	_____	_____	_____	_____
Day 55	_____	_____	_____	_____
Day 56	_____	_____	_____	_____

	Date	Walking	(Or . . . Swimming)	SUDAS
WEEK 9		45-minute walk	Add 30 seconds every day	Add 7 minutes per day
Day 57	_____	_____	_____	_____
Day 58	_____	_____	_____	_____
Day 59	_____	_____	_____	_____
Day 60	_____	_____	_____	_____
Day 61	_____	_____	_____	_____
Day 62	_____	_____	_____	_____
Day 63	_____	_____	_____	_____
WEEK 10		45-minute walk	Maintain	Add 8 minutes per day
Day 64	_____	_____	_____	_____
Day 65	_____	_____	_____	_____
Day 66	_____	_____	_____	_____
Day 67	_____	_____	_____	_____
Day 68	_____	_____	_____	_____
Day 69	_____	_____	_____	_____
Day 70	_____	_____	_____	_____
WEEK 11		45-minute walk	Maintain	Add 9 minutes per day
Day 71	_____	_____	_____	_____
Day 72	_____	_____	_____	_____
Day 73	_____	_____	_____	_____
Day 74	_____	_____	_____	_____
Day 75	_____	_____	_____	_____
Day 76	_____	_____	_____	_____
Day 77	_____	_____	_____	_____

	Date	Walking	(Or ... Swimming)	SUDAS
WEEK 12		45-minute walk	Maintain	Add 10 minutes per day
Day 78	_____	_____	_____	_____
Day 79	_____	_____	_____	_____
Day 80	_____	_____	_____	_____
Day 81	_____	_____	_____	_____
Day 82	_____	_____	_____	_____
Day 83	_____	_____	_____	_____
Day 84	_____	_____	_____	_____

Category 3: Slightly disabled
Recovery Progress Report for

_____

	Date	Walking	(Or . . . Swimming)	SUDAS
WEEK 1		Add 1 minute per day	Add 1 minute per day	Add 1 minute per day
Day 1	_____	_____	_____	_____
Day 2	_____	_____	_____	_____
Day 3	_____	_____	_____	_____
Day 4	_____	_____	_____	_____
Day 5	_____	_____	_____	_____
Day 6	_____	_____	_____	_____
Day 7	_____	_____	_____	_____
WEEK 2		Add 2 minutes per day	Add 1 minute per day	Add 2 minutes per day
Day 8	_____	_____	_____	_____
Day 9	_____	_____	_____	_____
Day 10	_____	_____	_____	_____
Day 11	_____	_____	_____	_____
Day 12	_____	_____	_____	_____
Day 13	_____	_____	_____	_____
Day 14	_____	_____	_____	_____

	Date	Walking	(Or . . . Swimming)	SUDAS
WEEK 3		Add 3 minutes per day (Max. Walk: 60 minutes)	Add 30 seconds every day	Add 3 minutes per day
Day 15	_____	_____	_____	_____
Day 16	_____	_____	_____	_____
Day 17	_____	_____	_____	_____
Day 18	_____	_____	_____	_____
Day 19	_____	_____	_____	_____
Day 20	_____	_____	_____	_____
Day 21	_____	_____	_____	_____
WEEK 4		60-minute walk	Maintain time	Add 4 minutes per day
Day 22	_____	_____	_____	_____
Day 23	_____	_____	_____	_____
Day 24	_____	_____	_____	_____
Day 25	_____	_____	_____	_____
Day 26	_____	_____	_____	_____
Day 27	_____	_____	_____	_____
Day 28	_____	_____	_____	_____
WEEK 5		60-minute walk	Add 30 seconds per day	Add 4 minutes per day
Day 29	_____	_____	_____	_____
Day 30	_____	_____	_____	_____
Day 31	_____	_____	_____	_____
Day 32	_____	_____	_____	_____
Day 33	_____	_____	_____	_____
Day 34	_____	_____	_____	_____
Day 35	_____	_____	_____	_____

	Date	Walking	(Or . . . Swimming)	SUDAS
WEEK 6		60-minute walk	Maintain	Add 5 minutes per day
Day 36	_____	_____	_____	_____
Day 37	_____	_____	_____	_____
Day 38	_____	_____	_____	_____
Day 39	_____	_____	_____	_____
Day 40	_____	_____	_____	_____
Day 41	_____	_____	_____	_____
Day 42	_____	_____	_____	_____
WEEK 7		60-minute walk	Maintain	Add 6 minutes per day
Day 43	_____	_____	_____	_____
Day 44	_____	_____	_____	_____
Day 45	_____	_____	_____	_____
Day 46	_____	_____	_____	_____
Day 47	_____	_____	_____	_____
Day 48	_____	_____	_____	_____
Day 49	_____	_____	_____	_____
WEEK 8		60-minute walk	Maintain	Add 7 minutes per day
Day 50	_____	_____	_____	_____
Day 51	_____	_____	_____	_____
Day 52	_____	_____	_____	_____
Day 53	_____	_____	_____	_____
Day 54	_____	_____	_____	_____
Day 55	_____	_____	_____	_____
Day 56	_____	_____	_____	_____

	Date	Walking	(Or ... Swimming)	SUDAS
WEEK 9		60-minute walk	Add 30 seconds per day	Add 8 minutes per day
Day 57	_____	_____	_____	_____
Day 58	_____	_____	_____	_____
Day 59	_____	_____	_____	_____
Day 60	_____	_____	_____	_____
Day 61	_____	_____	_____	_____
Day 62	_____	_____	_____	_____
Day 63	_____	_____	_____	_____
WEEK 10		60-minute walk	30 minutes maximum	Add 9 minutes per day
Day 64	_____	_____	_____	_____
Day 65	_____	_____	_____	_____
Day 66	_____	_____	_____	_____
Day 67	_____	_____	_____	_____
Day 68	_____	_____	_____	_____
Day 69	_____	_____	_____	_____
Day 70	_____	_____	_____	_____
WEEK 11		60-minute walk	30 minutes maximum	Add 10 minutes per day
Day 71	_____	_____	_____	_____
Day 72	_____	_____	_____	_____
Day 73	_____	_____	_____	_____
Day 74	_____	_____	_____	_____
Day 75	_____	_____	_____	_____
Day 76	_____	_____	_____	_____
Day 77	_____	_____	_____	_____

	Date	Walking	(Or . . . Swimming)	SUDAS
WEEK 12		60-minute walk	30 minutes maximum	Add 11 minutes per day
Day 78	_____	_____	_____	_____
Day 79	_____	_____	_____	_____
Day 80	_____	_____	_____	_____
Day 81	_____	_____	_____	_____
Day 82	_____	_____	_____	_____
Day 83	_____	_____	_____	_____
Day 84	_____	_____	_____	_____

Category 4: Occasionally incapacitated
Recovery Progress Report for

_____

	Date	Walking	(Or ... Swimming)	SUDAS
WEEK 1		Add 2 minutes per day	Add 1 minute per day	Add 2 minutes per day
Day 1	_____	_____	_____	_____
Day 2	_____	_____	_____	_____
Day 3	_____	_____	_____	_____
Day 4	_____	_____	_____	_____
Day 5	_____	_____	_____	_____
Day 6	_____	_____	_____	_____
Day 7	_____	_____	_____	_____
WEEK 2		Add 3 minutes per day (Max. walk: 60 minutes)	Add 1 minute per day	Add 3 minutes per day
Day 8	_____	_____	_____	_____
Day 9	_____	_____	_____	_____
Day 10	_____	_____	_____	_____
Day 11	_____	_____	_____	_____
Day 12	_____	_____	_____	_____
Day 13	_____	_____	_____	_____
Day 14	_____	_____	_____	_____

	Date	Walking	(Or . . . Swimming)	SUDAS
WEEK 3		60 minutes maximum	Add 30 seconds per day	Add 4 minutes per day
Day 15	_____	_____	_____	_____
Day 16	_____	_____	_____	_____
Day 17	_____	_____	_____	_____
Day 18	_____	_____	_____	_____
Day 19	_____	_____	_____	_____
Day 20	_____	_____	_____	_____
Day 21	_____	_____	_____	_____
WEEK 4		60-minute walk	Add 30 seconds per day	Add 5 minutes per day
Day 22	_____	_____	_____	_____
Day 23	_____	_____	_____	_____
Day 24	_____	_____	_____	_____
Day 25	_____	_____	_____	_____
Day 26	_____	_____	_____	_____
Day 27	_____	_____	_____	_____
Day 28	_____	_____	_____	_____
WEEK 5		60-minute walk	Add 30 seconds (Max. 35 minutes)	Add 6 minutes per day
Day 29	_____	_____	_____	_____
Day 30	_____	_____	_____	_____
Day 31	_____	_____	_____	_____
Day 32	_____	_____	_____	_____
Day 33	_____	_____	_____	_____
Day 34	_____	_____	_____	_____
Day 35	_____	_____	_____	_____

	Date	Walking	(Or . . . Swimming)	SUDAS
WEEK 6		60-minute walk	35 minutes maximum	Add 7 minutes per day
Day 36	_____	_____	_____	_____
Day 37	_____	_____	_____	_____
Day 38	_____	_____	_____	_____
Day 39	_____	_____	_____	_____
Day 40	_____	_____	_____	_____
Day 41	_____	_____	_____	_____
Day 42	_____	_____	_____	_____
WEEK 7		60-minute walk	35 minutes maximum	Add 8 minutes per day
Day 43	_____	_____	_____	_____
Day 44	_____	_____	_____	_____
Day 45	_____	_____	_____	_____
Day 46	_____	_____	_____	_____
Day 47	_____	_____	_____	_____
Day 48	_____	_____	_____	_____
Day 49	_____	_____	_____	_____
WEEK 8		60-minute walk	35 minutes maximum	Add 9 minutes per day
Day 50	_____	_____	_____	_____
Day 51	_____	_____	_____	_____
Day 52	_____	_____	_____	_____
Day 53	_____	_____	_____	_____
Day 54	_____	_____	_____	_____
Day 55	_____	_____	_____	_____
Day 56	_____	_____	_____	_____

	Date	Walking	(Or . . . Swimming)	SUDAS
WEEK 9		60-minute walk	35 minutes maximum	Add 10 minutes per day
Day 57	_____	_____	_____	_____
Day 58	_____	_____	_____	_____
Day 59	_____	_____	_____	_____
Day 60	_____	_____	_____	_____
Day 61	_____	_____	_____	_____
Day 62	_____	_____	_____	_____
Day 63	_____	_____	_____	_____
WEEK 10		60-minute walk	35 minutes maximum	Add 11 minutes per day
Day 64	_____	_____	_____	_____
Day 65	_____	_____	_____	_____
Day 66	_____	_____	_____	_____
Day 67	_____	_____	_____	_____
Day 68	_____	_____	_____	_____
Day 69	_____	_____	_____	_____
Day 70	_____	_____	_____	_____
WEEK 11		60-minute walk	35 minutes maximum	Add 12 minutes per day
Day 71	_____	_____	_____	_____
Day 72	_____	_____	_____	_____
Day 73	_____	_____	_____	_____
Day 74	_____	_____	_____	_____
Day 75	_____	_____	_____	_____
Day 76	_____	_____	_____	_____
Day 77	_____	_____	_____	_____

	Date	Walking	(Or ... Swimming)	SUDAS
WEEK 12		60-minute walk	35 minutes maximum	Add 13 minutes per day
Day 78	____	____	____	____
Day 79	____	____	____	____
Day 80	____	____	____	____
Day 81	____	____	____	____
Day 82	____	____	____	____
Day 83	____	____	____	____
Day 84	____	____	____	____

Category 5: Functional but in some pain
most of the time
Recovery Progress Report for

_____

	Date	Walking	(Or ... Swimming)	SUDAS
WEEK 1		Add 3 minutes per day	Add 1 minute per day	Add 3 minutes per day
Day 1	_____	_____	_____	_____
Day 2	_____	_____	_____	_____
Day 3	_____	_____	_____	_____
Day 4	_____	_____	_____	_____
Day 5	_____	_____	_____	_____
Day 6	_____	_____	_____	_____
Day 7	_____	_____	_____	_____
WEEK 2		Add 5 minutes per day (Max. 60 minutes)	Add 1 minute per day	Add 5 minutes per day
Day 8	_____	_____	_____	_____
Day 9	_____	_____	_____	_____
Day 10	_____	_____	_____	_____
Day 11	_____	_____	_____	_____
Day 12	_____	_____	_____	_____
Day 13	_____	_____	_____	_____
Day 14	_____	_____	_____	_____

	Date	Walking	(Or ... Swimming)	SUDAS
WEEK 3		60-minutes maximum	Add 30 seconds per day	Add 7 minutes per day
Day 15	_____	_____	_____	_____
Day 16	_____	_____	_____	_____
Day 17	_____	_____	_____	_____
Day 18	_____	_____	_____	_____
Day 19	_____	_____	_____	_____
Day 20	_____	_____	_____	_____
Day 21	_____	_____	_____	_____
WEEK 4		60-minutes maximum	Add 30 seconds per day	Add 9 minutes per day
Day 22	_____	_____	_____	_____
Day 23	_____	_____	_____	_____
Day 24	_____	_____	_____	_____
Day 25	_____	_____	_____	_____
Day 26	_____	_____	_____	_____
Day 27	_____	_____	_____	_____
Day 28	_____	_____	_____	_____
WEEK 5		60-minutes maximum	Add 30 seconds per day	Add 11 minutes per day
Day 29	_____	_____	_____	_____
Day 30	_____	_____	_____	_____
Day 31	_____	_____	_____	_____
Day 32	_____	_____	_____	_____
Day 33	_____	_____	_____	_____
Day 34	_____	_____	_____	_____
Day 35	_____	_____	_____	_____

	Date	*Walking*	*(Or . . . Swimming)*	*SUDAS*
WEEK 6		60-minutes maximum	Add 40 seconds (Max. 40 minutes)	Add 13 minutes per day
Day 36	_____	_____	_____	_____
Day 37	_____	_____	_____	_____
Day 38	_____	_____	_____	_____
Day 39	_____	_____	_____	_____
Day 40	_____	_____	_____	_____
Day 41	_____	_____	_____	_____
Day 42	_____	_____	_____	_____
WEEK 7		60-minutes maximum	Add 40 seconds	Add 15 minutes per day
Day 43	_____	_____	_____	_____
Day 44	_____	_____	_____	_____
Day 45	_____	_____	_____	_____
Day 46	_____	_____	_____	_____
Day 47	_____	_____	_____	_____
Day 48	_____	_____	_____	_____
Day 49	_____	_____	_____	_____
WEEK 8		60-minutes maximum	Add 40 seconds	Add 17 minutes per day
Day 50	_____	_____	_____	_____
Day 51	_____	_____	_____	_____
Day 52	_____	_____	_____	_____
Day 53	_____	_____	_____	_____
Day 54	_____	_____	_____	_____
Day 55	_____	_____	_____	_____
Day 56	_____	_____	_____	_____

9

Instant Relief: The Best and Safest Non-Prescription Pain-Stoppers

In this chapter we look at what you can do for yourself to stop or alleviate pain. The best way to stop chronic pain yourself is to follow a multi-faceted, gradual, long-term programme, like the one described in this book. However, the self-help therapies in this chapter are aimed at the short term – simple steps you can take *right now* to get temporary relief.

"Temporary relief" isn't meant to minimize the good you can do for yourself. *Any* relief from pain is a godsend. It's critical for the reprieve it brings you, and it is equally important for enabling long-term progress to take place.

The techniques in this chapter – gleaned from the most frequently made suggestions of survey participants – are directed toward the following goals:

1. To enable you to feel there is always hope for pain relief, even if your chronic pain condition takes a downward turn and you feel as if you won't be able to go on unless there is relief in sight.
2. To keep you calm and hopeful at your worst moments – no small feat, especially given the unpredictability of chronic pain symptoms from hour to hour and day to day.
3. To give you options for obtaining relief from pain. If there were one simple way to relieve pain that worked for everyone – an incorrect assumption made by many self-proclaimed chronic pain gurus – this would be a very short

chapter. Here's an example of such a theory, entirely made-up and unreal. "Have you got a pain? Just squeeze your right earlobe for two seconds, pause one second, squeeze again for two seconds. Now repeat this procedure on your left earlobe." In just writing this example, I'm tempted to believe it myself, and I know it's invented and ridiculous! When you're in dire pain, it takes the greatest act of will not to swallow whole the latest panacea offered up by contemporary quacks. If it isn't "squeeze your earlobe", then it's "just change your attitude" or a "cure-all ointment" or even just send for a "new device with electromagnetic vibrations." When you're in pain, you dearly want to believe in any instant exit for that pain. Although there is no instant exit there are instantly usable options for stopping pain temporarily and they do work. You definitely want all of these options in your arsenal because, given the fanciful and ever-changing nature of chronic pain, what may work wonders for you on a Monday may not work at all on a Tuesday.

4. To give you a sense of new-found power over your ability to change your life for the better. The core issue in your life is relentless and intractable pain; if you can ease it, if you can do anything significant about it, you can easily feel: I can stop pain. Hence, I can get well and turn around my life! What's more, if you believe this, your mind may well help your body to recover fully from chronic pain. We don't know this to be true, but we do know that it can and does happen for some people.

In short, this chapter offers some small but significant pain-ending cures in this chapter – each based on what survey participants for this book consider to be the best self-help approaches available. Try to learn them and experiment with them, because there is no knowing which one or ones will work best for you at any given time.

INNER CUES – THE MOST POTENT PAIN-STOPPER OF ALL

Let's pretend for a moment that some technological wizard invented a chronic-pain device that you could wear on your wrist. To mask its real purpose, it is a watch as well as a magical pain-stopping device. It has the power to tell you precisely when you should stop doing a particular activity – with the ironclad guarantee that if you stopped at this particular moment you would halt pain before it could get started.

Sounds good? This "device" takes the form of your inner cues to pain. Here's how to recognize these inner cues:

• A perceptible shift from low-level pain (discomfort you can live with) to what we'll call flashing-amber pain: a caution light that tells you there is known agony ahead. Your inner voice may whisper to you: "That's enough; take a break." You may tell your inner voice: "Keep quiet" or "Go away". Sometimes you feel that you must go on. That's understandable. But it's important to understand this, too: if you stop when you are at your flashing-amber light, instead of waiting until your red light is on, and you do this consistently for weeks and months, you'll break out of the deep rut of chronic pain once and for all. Try to see the bigger picture of your recovery, and heed your inner cues.

• A new kind of pain that concerns you. Perhaps it's a pain you've never had before, or it's one you haven't had for a very long time, or it's a limiting pain that especially reminds you of your first few weeks or months of chronic pain. The pain may or not be particularly severe, but it is worrisome. When you have this kind of pain, take a break. Use one of the pain-stopping techniques below. Ease your pain and your worry – right away.

• You feel fatigued. Everything starts to ache. It would be difficult to say where your pain is, because it's in large areas – your back, buttocks, hips and upper legs, for example. Whatever it takes to ease this feeling, do it.

• You hear two voices at once. No, you're not hearing things. The first voice is yours. It says to stop what you're doing and take care of yourself. The second voice is "others" – people in your life, or books that you've read, or doctors that you've seen. This second voice feels accusatory. It uses phrases such as "Oh, c'mon, the pain isn't all that bad," or "Stop being such a wimp" or "Quit spoiling everyone else's good time." This is a good time to remind yourself: no one else is going to make you well. You are going to have to do that for yourself. You are the only human being on this planet who can give yourself an accurate reading of how you feel. It is utterly essential that you believe in yourself. As tempting as it for all of us to hope that a god-like expert will make us well, most of us get well by learning to hone and rely on our own judgment..

TWO POSITIONS THAT EASE MOST CHRONIC PAIN WITHIN MINUTES

1. **On your back with feet up.** This position has been recommended in numerous books, with slight but significant variations. According to this book's survey participants, the best position for easing pain is lying on a thick gym mat or a few folded blankets, with your arms at your sides, a pillow under your neck and head, and your knees bent and your feet propped up on a low chair. Take deep breaths from your belly, exhale through your mouth. Try to *feel* yourself relax. Try playing your favourite music, softly, as you lie like this. Focus on the beauty or the rhythm of the music, rather than on your body. Try to "be the music" rather than being your physical body. If getting down to or lying on the floor is too difficult for you, lie on your bed. Instead of propping your feet on a low chair, bend your knees and prop your feet on two or three thick pillows.
2. **The foetal position.** The position described above bothers the lower backs or hips of a small minority of people. If you're one of these people, lie in a foetal position on your bed, with a pillow under your neck and head, and a pillow between your knees. Follow the rest of the suggestions above about taking deep breaths and trying to feel relaxed. Within several minutes, you should feel noticeable relief throughout your entire body.

THE MAGIC OF KNEADING AND ICING

Is your lower back aching? Do the outsides of your thighs hurt? Are your buttocks in spasm? Your shoulders bothering you? Your lower legs giving you trouble?

Use the kneader/roller that you were designed with at birth. I refer to the heel of your palm – the 2–3-inch fleshy area just below your thumb, extending down to your wrist. Kneading with this flexible but firm surface helped many of this book's survey participants to stop muscle spasms and pain. After kneading, applying an ice pack or large-area ice hydrocollator (for moist heat or cold treatments) to the area straight away keeps spasms from returning and can provide further pain relief.

Here are more specific tips for this knead/ice method.

- **Outsides of thighs.** Sit in a chair. Start kneading one leg just above the knee, using a circular motion for a few seconds in each spot. Work your way in this fashion toward the fleshy spot just under your hip bone and give that a little attention while you're at it. Now repeat this process, bearing down with more pressure, but stopping short of increasing your pain. Finish this leg by resting on your side in bed and placing ice packs for two minutes on the painful areas that you have just worked on. Then repeat this process for the other leg.
- **Lower legs.** Use the same approach described above. For greater comfort, prop up one foot on a stool before you begin, and work on that leg first. Then repeat for the other leg.
- **Lower back.** Most people can reach around to knead their lower backs while they're sitting in a chair or lying on their side in bed. (If you can't get enough leverage, or if you can't reach far enough around, you'll need someone to do the kneading for you.) Draw an imaginary line in your mind around the area of your lower back that bothers you most – one side at a time. Start to knead in the centre of that area. Spend at least two minutes in this first spot, kneading gently at first with a small circular motion, then

pressing harder if this doesn't increase your pain. Now move outward from the centre of your pain, giving each area a minute of kneading. Finally, apply ice packs to the area for two minutes.

- **Buttocks.** Use the same approach described immediately above for "Lower back".
- **Shoulders.** Use your right hand to reach over your left shoulder. Grasp your left shoulder blade with the fingertips of your right hand and knead slowly in small circles for a minute or two. Apply an ice pack for a minute. Then work on the other shoulder.

GIVING PAIN THE THUMB

Sometimes, an area of pain is smaller than the tip of your thumb. It tends to radiate pain, constantly or intermittently, is usually tender to the touch and feels like a tiny bump or nodule in an area of muscle. "Triggerpoint" is the word most often used to describe these tiny sources of pain that radiate to much larger areas and can cause great discomfort.

To work on an area, get into the most comfortable position you can – lying, sitting or reclining. Apply your thumb tip – the area directly behind your thumbnail – to the painful area. Gently apply pressure, staying in that spot while moving your thumb tip in a circular motion. Every ten seconds or so, press down directly on the spot as if you were trying to flatten it out.

(*A note of caution*: This is the only "pain-stopper" in this book that will temporarily cause more pain for virtually everyone. There's no way around this; the area is so tender to the touch. If you have any doubt at all about wanting to try this technique, don't. Instead, you might consider getting the same kind of treatment from a licensed shiatsu massage therapist, or from a physiatrist (doctor of physical and rehabilitative medicine), who uses an injection instead of a pinpoint massage.)

If you're using this treatment on yourself, apply an ice pack for two minutes immediately afterward.

HOUSEHOLD OBJECTS THAT "ROLL OUT" PAIN

Areas that trigger and radiate pain can be just out of your reach. If this is the case, and you want to be able to do something yourself to cool down your pain, try "rolling it out" while lying down.

For example, let's say you have a painful area under one of your shoulder blades. Find yourself a "roller" device. It can be a wooden or plastic acupressure roller sold by backache supply stores, equipped with two wheels, each about three inches high, attached to a wooden rod looking something like a tiny barbell with ends (wheels) that roll. Or it could be a massage device with "bumps" that you can press into the affected area. Alternatively you can improvise: try anything from a salt mill to a ketchup bottle (top tightly on!!) to a small rolling pin. Using our example of a painful area just below your shoulder blade, lie on the floor and place the object under you, right on that area, and relax your weight on it. If it feels too painful, stop immediately. If the counterpressure feels good, even if a bit achy, squirm or roll around on it – as if you were trying to roll out the painful area (which probably feels like it has small knots or nodules in it). Alternately, just let the pressure work on the area for a few minutes, without moving around too much. When you've finished, apply an ice pack for two minutes immediately afterward.

Any area of the upper back is a good bet for this self-therapy. It's easy to shift your weight onto painful places, and you will be able to apply various levels of weight.

What about your lower back? Some survey participants used the roller technique on areas of their lower back with success; others said that putting a roller under them caused them to arch their back and negate any positive effects. Some value was also found from rolling on a painful soft tissue area near the hips or sides of the legs.

(*A note of caution*: if you experiment with putting a roller under your hips, or under the outsides of your thighs, be especially careful. Placing too much weight on these spots can lead to more pain.)

OVER-THE-COUNTER PAIN RELIEVER – ASPIRIN

Although it has definite drawbacks and risks which we'll review here, old-fashioned aspirin, now a century old as a commercial remedy, was still the top choice of survey participants for over-the-counter (non-prescription) pain relievers, with acetaminophen (Tylenol, for example) or ibuprofen (Nurofen) a distant second. In fact, aspirin was so good that survey participants with arthritis rated it as effective as any prescription drug.

Nevertheless, it is important to check with your healthcare practitioner before using aspirin as a treatment for chronic pain. If it is suitable for you, you'll want specific advice about how much to take, when, and for how long. Be warned, though, aspirin can play havoc with your stomach and it can thin your blood, a hazard for some people. And there are other side effects for some individuals, including ringing in the ears.

On the plus side, aspirin is the only major over-the-counter drug that delivers both anti-inflammatory and analgesic potency. Relative to other drugs, it is inexpensive and you can even use it prophylactically. For example, if you're going to be doing something strenuous, taking aspirin an hour beforehand can stop pain before it starts. Again, though, do consult your healthcare provider about using aspirin for any purpose.

GELS, CREAMS AND LOTIONS

If a magical potion exists in a bottle or tube, the survey participants for this book didn't find it. They rated all gels, creams and lotions at or below the level of a placebo (sugar pill or make-believe medication). This isn't to say that many didn't get temporary and important relief from these substances. Indeed, one in three users got temporary relief – the same per centage as the average placebo effect. By all means, if you want to try products that get more blood to painful areas (some of these products also have a brief numbing effect), do. As long as you know the product is safe for topical application, and that any relief will be temporary, go ahead and experiment.

INCREASED HYDRATION

Less than a dozen people in the research for this book recommended drinking more water as a way to decrease pain. There is some indication that drinking eight to twelve tall glasses of water a day will help flush away the waste matter from muscle use, and perhaps lessen pain. If you have incidents of acute pain, mixed with your chronic pain, you might want to give the hydration approach a try.

ICE MASSAGE

You'll get the shivers just thinking about this one. But you might also get some relief. Put about a half dozen ice cubes in a plastic bag or wrap. Grip this "ice ball" and rub it briskly over the painful area. Keep the ice moving, never stopping for more than a second or two in any one place. Massage slightly beyond the painful area in all directions. Keep this going for about ninety seconds, but do not exceed ninety seconds because of the risk of frostbite.

MAGNET THERAPY

Whenever there's pain or illness, and any degree of uncertainty about the path to wellness, magical cure fads appear on a regular basis. Most of them come and go, without anyone ever knowing exactly how well they worked, if at all. Pyramids were hot a decade ago. DMSO (see p. 189) was a sure bet for all pains and sprains before that. Vitamins C and E had their run. Calcium had some play. And now we have magnets.

Will wearing magnets over a painful area help you? Based on the relatively small number of participants in this survey who tried magnet therapy – fifty-two chronic pain sufferers – gains made failed to exceed the placebo level. In other words, only one third of users reported progress.

10

How to Be Your Own Chronic Pain Expert

Who is the chronic pain expert most likely to help you improve your life from this day forward? Who is best qualified to come up with pain-relieving strategies based on the routines and details of *your* daily life? *You are this expert.*

This chapter will show you how to use the invaluable knowledge that only *you* have about yourself, for the greatest benefit. The strategies and insights for achieving these gains represent the wisdom of recovered chronic pain sufferers. They are easy to apply. Keeping them in mind at all times will help you to feel that you really *do* have a substantial degree of power over your pain.

HOW TO GET STARTED

Prepare yourself for a temporary career change! In your new role as sharp-eyed sleuth, you're going to discover simple but effective changes you can make, twenty-four hours a day, to relieve your pain and put more vitality into your life.

All you need to do is to observe yourself for a single day and night and follow the guidelines below. Attend to yourself as closely as you would observe a loved one in constant pain.

SLEEPING AND WAKING UP

Mattresses – select firm, shun extra-firm
The common wisdom that the firmer the mattress, the less the discomfort, is not so wise. An extra-firm mattress is especially painful for most people with osteoarthritis of the spine or people with hip pain. A moderately firm mattress, with enough

yield in it to let your body's weight "make a dent," is best for most people. Firmer than this and you might as well be lying on a foam-covered board – a bad idea for most people with back, hip and leg pain.

• *Futons* are too hard for most chronic pain sufferers. And you don't get the gently yielding "give" needed to keep your body well-aligned.

• *Water beds* have no relevance for most of us. The most common complaint about them: you are not in control of many of your movements in bed – the water in the mattress is! In bed, you definitely want to feel in control of when you move and when you don't!

• *Mushy mattresses* – those that sag into a valley shape and distort the natural contours of our prone bodies – are harmful. If you get stuck on one of these mattresses while travelling, try to put a board under it. If there is no board available, and you have no other alternative, put the mattress on the floor and sleep there for a night. Before you do this, though, read the tip immediately below!

This one will floor you

About one in fifty chronic pain sufferers from this book's research showed great enthusiasm for sleeping on the floor. "I had a terrible back ache," a typical floor-lover told me, "so I slept on the floor, still do it and I'm fine." For most of us, though, sleeping on the floor is not so comfortable. It puts too much pressure on our muscles and joints. It's too draughty, especially in winter. And it's too tough on the knees to get up and down from, especially for people who wake several times in the night and need to get in and out of bed.

Position yourself for sleep

Is your favourite position for sleep the best sleeping position for your chronic pain? If it isn't, can you change a less-than-ideal sleeping posture that has been a favourite of yours for as long you first clutched a stuffed toy at night? The consensus of most chronic pain sufferers is that it's worth a try.

• The *foetal position* – lying on your side, knees bent, with a pillow between them to ease strain by aligning your lower body with your upper body – is the most comfortable position for most pain sufferers. The one notable exception is people with hip pain or hip numbness.

- *Tummy sleepers* tend to arch their backs too much and suffer worse pain as a result. If you feel you must sleep on your stomach, because you've been doing it since you were a baby, try a small pillow under your *lower* abdomen. This should lessen the extent that you arch your back. If using a pillow doesn't feel comfortable, try putting your arms and hands beneath you, just inside your hips and inner thighs. (Caution: for some people, this position causes numbness in the arms and hands.)

- How about *sleeping on your back*? About one in three chronic pain sufferers sleeps this way with good results. If this feels good for you, you might try making yourself more comfortable by placing a medium-firm pillow or foam wedge under your knees.

- Don't worry about *winding up in the "wrong" position* once you're asleep and shifting around in bed. There's no way to avoid moving around at night. If you happen to wind up in an unfavourable position that wakes you, just shift back again.

    If you're concerned about keeping a pillow in place between or under your knees during the middle of the night, you can attach a pillow to your knees with a Velcro strap. Or you can buy a pillow that is designed to stay in the desired position.

Loosen up in bed

A chronic pain sufferer told me recently, "I'm so grateful for every new day in my life that, upon awakening, I bolt upright immediately and thank God." She added, unhappily, "But this makes my back hurt!" Every morning, this eighty-one-year-old woman would take a deep breath and go from lying flat to sitting bolt upright. A rather astonishing feat requiring excellent abdominal muscles! And a fairly ruinous thing to do to a body first thing in the morning!

- *Start your day gently*. If you're stiff, or if your pain is at its worst first thing in the morning, try limbering up *before* you leave the bed. Here are two ways to do this:

1. Have a heated pad (moist heat, preferably) at the ready and apply it to your most painful areas.
2. Do what I informally term the "wiggle-waggle" – a playful and leisurely way to begin the day.

This is one description of a wiggle-waggle routine that is enjoyed by more than 100 chronic pain sufferers who participated in the survey for this book. Feel free to substitute your own gentle motions for the ones mentioned.

* Lie on your back with your legs straight out in front of you. (If lying this way bothers you, skip this motion and proceed to below.) Start moving your body. Begin with your feet, by wiggling them one at a time.
* Slide one heel a few feet toward you until your knee is fully bent; then slide back again. Wiggle that leg slowly. Now do the same movements with the other heel and leg.
* Gently clench and unclench your thighs and relax for a few seconds.
* Lying on your back with your knees up, feet flat on the mattress, use your abdominal muscles to arch your pelvis upward while simultaneously flattening the small of your back into the mattress. Hold for one second. (If all this sounds overly complicated, simply focus on flattening the space between the small of your back and the mattress. Stick your hand, palm down, into the space to check how you're doing.
* Take a five-count deep breath through your belly (you'll be able to see your belly rise when you "breathe through your belly") and exhale for a five-count. Now, without straining or forcing, stretch your arms toward the ceiling. Relax for a few seconds, then shrug your shoulders . . . slowly.
* Final muscle movement: smile. It's difficult being in pain, but you're working purposefully toward improving your

life. These seemingly little steps you're taking can add up to big progress over just a few weeks. Keep going. You're doing well!

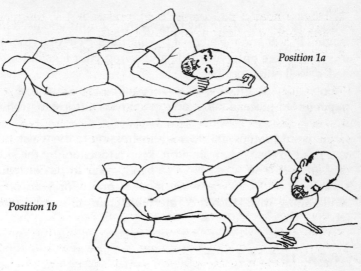

Position 1a

Position 1b

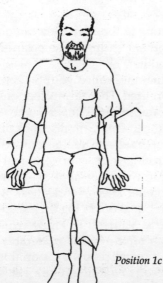

Rise, shine and dress in comfort

The *least stressful way to get out of bed* in the morning, or after a nap, is to start on your side. (**Position 1a.**) Place your palms down on the mattress. (**Position 1b.**) In one motion, press down with your palms, move your legs off the bed and sit up on the edge of the bed. (**Position 1c.**)

Position 1c

- Is it difficult for you to *get dressed* – especially to put on socks or stockings, underwear, trousers and shoes? If so, try to find an easier way. Try getting dressed to the waist while lying in bed.

  To get back into bed, simply reverse the motions you used for leaving it. a) Sit on the edge of the mattress. b) In one smooth motion, recline onto your side and swing your legs onto the bed. c) Roll onto your back.

  Concerned about dirty shoes on your bed? Just use a newspaper or old piece of fabric on top of your bedding to protect it.

- If you would rather sit down while dressing to the waist, but you need to ease the strain a bit, keep a footstool by the side of your bed. You won't have to bend so far to put on your shoes and socks. If you want more support for your back while doing this, sit in a comfortable chair and use a footstool.

GENERAL TIPS FOR SITTING

Sitting pretty

For some chronic pain sufferers, sitting is about all they can do when they're not lying down. For others, sitting is the position that gives them more pain than any other.

- Keep the small of your back – sometimes called your S-curve or lumbar curve – adequately supported. There are exceptions to every rule about sitting. For example, my wife, Pat, who is the illustrator and de facto editor-in-chief of this book in progress, cannot use a lumbar support when she sits. It makes her back feel horrible, thus ruling out every lumbar-supporting chair ever made. For Pat, a bench or stool, or a chair specially designed to let her sit on her knees, works best. In other words, don't feel odd or left out about being the exception to any rule in this book. Trust yourself to know what works for you. Buy a chair with a built-in (and, preferably, adjustable) lumbar support. Or use a small pillow or a portable lumbar support. Or, use anything soft or foldable, like a jacket or blanket or towel.

- Your knees should be as high, or slightly higher, than your hips. If you're sitting in a chair that slopes downward, and your knees are lower than your hips, use a footrest to raise your knees. Or, fold up anything soft and put it under the backs of your lower thighs and knees.

Sitting and working

- If you're working for any length of time at a table – writing, typing or drawing – raise your chair (or raise yourself in the chair) high enough so that the table you're working at is on the level of, or not much above waist level. If the table is higher than this, the effort it takes to keep your arms raised is likely to tire your back.
- Pull your chair close to the table. The more you have to reach your arms out in front of your body, the greater the strain on your back.

Sitting and driving

- If you're driving, and your back feels achey, pull your seat closer to the wheel. Another idea – safety permitting – is to drive with one hand on the wheel, the other arm relaxed in your lap. Do this for just a few seconds at a time; your back will thank you.
- Is the shape or angle of your car seat driving you crazy? If you're sitting in a bucket seat whose "bucket" slopes downward, causing the front "rim" of the seat to angle upward under your thighs, this position may cause aching hamstrings, numbing or a sharp pain in the back of one or both of your legs. To ease this discomfort, build up the lower, rear part of the bucket seat with dense foam rubber or evenly distributed towels.
- When you stop to take a rest break on a trip, experiment with slightly changing the angle of the back of your car seat. Move it forward or back a notch or two. Each time you take a rest break – once an hour is a must and the more breaks the better – change this tilt position slightly; the variety may help you feel more comfortable on a long trip.
- Use a lumbar support while you're driving.

- Consider using a full car seat – a lumbar back support that is attached to a base (seat) for your rear and thighs.
- Stretch out on the back seat during breaks. Don't be embarrassed about being seen lying down. Stretching out like this, in addition to walking around for a few minutes, can make all the difference.
- If you have someone to share the driving with, get into the passenger seat and lean it back all the way. Or, lean halfway back and either tuck your legs under you or prop your feet on the dashboard.

Sitting in public places

- At a concert hall, movie or theatre, try to get an aisle seat. This allows you to stretch your legs more. It also enables you to get up, take a break, and come back with minimum fuss and bother.
- Above all, when sitting starts to make your back or legs feel bad, get up and move around. A good rule of thumb: get up every thirty minutes and take a two-minute break from sitting. It's easy to get so absorbed in what you're doing, that you sit through mounting pain. Try not to let this happen. Set a clock if need be, but don't stay glued to your chair.
- If sitting is the most painful part of your life, and your activities are limited because of it, minimize your sitting for a month and proceed with this book's walking or swimming program, and stretch–strengthen exercise program. At the one-month mark, start sitting again – at a level that is 20% less than you could sit comfortably on your worst days. Increase this sitting time by five minutes a day. In just two months, at this relatively slow pace of progress, you'll be able to sit five additional hours a day.

LIFTING
Dos and don'ts

- Contrary to popular notions, most people don't injure their backs lifting heavy weights. Of course, some people *do* get hurt this way, but most of us injure ourselves in, through no fault of our own, simply by *reaching* to lift something. We never actually get to lift! A tissue falls to the floor . . . we reach to get it – everything locks up and we can't move. We reach for a pencil, a speck of dust, the cuff of our trousers, a glass on a bedside table, and it's a week before we can move freely again.

- Bend your knees when you go to lift anything below your waist level. If your knees are in worse shape than your back, use a gripper to lift low-lying objects that weigh a few pounds or less.
- Reaching for high objects – those on a top shelf, for example – can arch the back and cause pain. Instead of reaching, stand on a safety-designed, firm-footing stool. If you can't manage getting onto a stool, get a friend to help you to move things around on your shelves, so that what you'll need the most on a daily basis is at eye level. For example, are your breakfast cereals or soups on the top shelf? If so, move them to a more comfortable waist level.
- How about lifting heavy objects? Don't if you can avoid it! When you must lift, get your body as close as possible to the object you're lifting. This is as important as bending your knees! The further away you are from what you're lifting, the greater the strain on your back.
- A lot of lifting goes on during food shopping. When taking food out of the shopping cart, or out of your car, get as close to the bag as possible and bend your knees. When you're carrying bags of food, try carrying one bag by a handle in each hand, with your arms hanging down – rather than clutching two bags against your chest or hips. When you're putting food away, place a chair or small table next to your fridge and use it for the food that goes onto lower food shelves. This way, you need bend only once to put fruits and vegetables into bins.
- On the subject of food shopping, just getting to and through the supermarket can be a problem, especially for women who carry shoulder bags loaded up with enough objects to challenge a weightlifter. Move your bag from shoulder to shoulder as often as you can. Better yet, switch from a shoulder bag to a backpack. Or, simply carry less.

STANDING

Buttocks in, pain out

Is there a person over the age of five who hasn't been told more than once to "stand up straight?" Close your ears! Or at least change your definition of what "stand up straight" means. The old military notion of chest out, chin up and body ramrod rigid is a prescription for either making the rank of General or being admitted into a general hospital with back pain!

- Do you know where your backside is? It shouldn't be backing away from you, thereby arching your back when you're standing around. It should be "tucked in." Get up for a moment and stand the way you usually do. Now, tilt your pelvic area an inch or two forward (so that the top of the pelvis moves back), and you will find your backside moves down into a more vertical position. Now you know what "tucked in" means! *This is the single most important adjustment to posture for chronic pain sufferers.*

- Keep your head about you, too, when you're standing. Not cloud-gazing. Not downcast. More like you're contemplating a distant horizon. For a more specific idea of what this means, stand with your back against a wall, heels touching the wall. The back of your head, when you're looking straight ahead, should graze or almost touch the wall. Your shoulder blades also should touch or almost touch the wall. Your backside shouldn't – if it does, tilt your pelvis forwards as discussed above.

  Now move away from the wall. If you didn't pass all these check points, reread this section and practise some more. What you want to achieve is to stand properly without having to think about it. So, *do* think about it a lot when you practise, until it becomes second nature to you.

Two final points about standing. Have you ever heard anyone at a bar complain about a bad back? I'm definitely not recommending more drinking in bars, but the point is that putting a foot up on a lower bar rail, stair or stool *does* ease lower back pain. So don't start drinking. But do find ways to shift your weight. Slouch rather then standing ramrod straight and just move around as much as possible.

If you're on your feet for a long time, and you feel achey and have no place to sit or lie . . . lean against a wall. Position yourself about a foot away from a wall, with your feet about a foot apart. Now, flatten the small of your back against the wall, bend your knees, and slide down a little bit, then back up. Some chronic pain sufferers find this as useful as a short break lying prone.

Feet first!

If you feel weighed down by responsibilities, imagine how your feet feel! Treat them well, for it's critical that they be fully functioning.

- If you have *any* foot discomfort – a corn, bunion, ingrown nail, infection, structural problem – anything that could alter your gait or the way you stand, get professional treatment for it. There are instances, admittedly rare, where restoring feet to good health can completely eliminate chronic pain.

- Do you follow the widespread advice to change your shoes every day, so no single pair will become too sweaty – or smelly? Or do you kick off your shoes after a day's work and walk around barefoot or in slippers? Or, do you change from high heels or thick heels to low heels or no heels? If you answered "yes" to any of these questions, you're probably fine. But, there's a slight chance that changing what's under your feet every day is greatly aggravating and prolonging your chronic pain.

If you have a lot of leg or back pain, try this experiment for a week or two. If you wear high heels to start your day, or you if change shoes at night from a fairly built-up heel to slippers or bare feet, stop doing this temporarily. Rather than changing shoe heights, change instead to a fresh pair of the same model of shoe that you began the day with. According to this book's survey participants, there's about a one in twenty chance that you'll dramatically curb your chronic pain by walking on the same kind of shoe surface day in and day out.

Making adjustments from the feet up can work wonders in other ways, too. Do you have a limp when you walk? Is one leg substantially shorter than the other? (Slight differences in leg length are normal.) Four chronic pain sufferers surveyed for this book completely eliminated chronic pain by adding a lift to one shoe. Six more recovered by wearing prescribed arch supports.

PLANNING YOUR WAY OUT OF PAIN

If you reckon on having some pain at certain times, you can plan not to have that pain!

This idea of anticipating pain may sound odd to you or even negative. On the contrary, it's one of the healthiest things you can do for yourself. It means you are taking responsibility for your condition, without blaming yourself. And, most of all, it encourages the hope of finding new ways to cope with chronic pain.

For years, Todd Becker, a fibromyalgia sufferer and attorney, suffered a nightmarish ride home from work. He would feel tired in late afternoon, in pain by 5 p.m. and filled with misery until he could lie down after he got home at seven, often too distraught to eat dinner. All that ended when Todd decided to shut down work for fifteen minutes at 4 p.m. every day, except when major meetings took priority, in order to do something about his pain before it did something to him. Giving himself this break worked wonders, turning his evenings from discomfort to pleasure.

So, plan your day around your most painful times. It's possible that the break from pain you'll give yourself could end these painful times forever – and it's even possible that you could get well enough to be able to give up mandatory rest breaks.

It takes "attitude" to banish pain

"Attitude", in this instance, doesn't mean merely thinking positively or being cheerful about chronic pain. More to the point, it means having a consistently positive approach toward your own priorities – treating yourself in a kind and thoughtful way on a daily basis, so you'll be more likely to do some good things for yourself.

Learn to use put yourself first until you have recovery well underway:

- Pour scorn on the *myth of "no pain, no gain"*. If this maxim about exercise were true for chronic pain sufferers – given their constant pain – then they would all be gaining a great deal and be completely well! This isn't the case, so please forget the need for pain in order to have gain.

  For the most part, the route to gain in chronic pain comes from the *absence* of pain. "Less pain, more gain" is a better maxim to follow. Do small kindnesses for yourself on a daily basis. Take breaks when you need them. Applaud your own heroic efforts in getting through another day as a chronic pain sufferer.

  The notion that you have to be hard-nosed about pain, and endure the most pain possible every day, is the myth that held back hundreds of this book's chronic pain sufferers. I know about this notion first-hand. I've been there. There were activities I wasn't ready for that I used to do – to my detriment. There was a wedding I couldn't bear to miss, a heavy object I had to lift when I couldn't tolerate having to ask for help; spending the night on my feet after my wife gave birth, in order to make sure that she got proper medical attention. On the lighter side, even fun activities like joining a game of pick-up basketball or doing gardening can be irresistible, albeit harmful if you're not ready for them.

  Going through pain is sometimes necessary, but too much of it will make it impossible to restore yourself to fitness and health. Only reprieve from pain can lead to further and more pain-free times. At some point, you have to put yourself first *now* in order to put other people first in the future.

- *Take a "no-prisoners" attitude.* Chronic pain sufferers suffer the indignity of having a disease that is too often seen as "nothing wrong". They are dismissed more times than a tele-marketing salesperson. Blamed for their own hell, and some-times even accused of wanting this hell.

It's time to fight back. Tell people what you have – chronic pain disease – so you can help them to be informed, and insist that doctors take you seriously. If they don't get it, and some won't, ask to see a different doctor.

* *Look at your natural fear of relapse.* Most chronic pain sufferers remember in vivid detail – where they were, who they were with, what they were saying – when they were at their worst level of physical pain. It may have been the time of the injury that first felled them and ignited years of chronic pain. It may have been the first time they couldn't button their shirt themselves. Or, the first time they couldn't sit through a movie or show or school play. Whatever that moment, we fear going back to it, or even sinking below it. Relapsing is a fearful thought, but one that is difficult to stop thinking about.

  The fear of relapsing – never the cause of chronic pain, but the result of it – can limit the extent that you dare to make progress. The only safeguard against it is timed, gradated, step-by-step progress. Baby-step progress if you will – the kind that takes time but gets you there feeling terrific about yourself, the kind of fitness that you develop safely and soundly through walking (or swimming), stretching/strengthening exercises and mind–body strategies.

* Take a candid look at the *inevitable stress and emotional prob-lems brought on by chronic pain.* Everyone alive suffers from stress in varying degrees. And, most assuredly, everyone who has to spend just one week in bed suffers stress. People who are bedridden for just a week worry about their jobs and families. They fear they won't get well quickly. They may even wonder whether they brought on their illness. Now change this scenario to suffering for one year or ten years with chronic pain disease. Every human being on this planet would experience stress and anxiety from being in this situation!

Does this mean that you should run to a psychotherapist if you have chronic pain? No, but it does mean that you have to accept the hell you've been through, and the impact on your mind, and consider whether it might be helpful for you to talk to a professional.

After listening to more than a thousand chronic pain sufferers discuss the emotional turmoil resulting from their chronic pain, three realities are clear:

1. Chronic pain takes a heavy emotional toll.
2. Psychotherapy helps most chronic pain sufferers, lightening their emotional load and sometimes helping them to accelerate their physical progress.
3. It is painful for chronic pain sufferers to sort out the physical and emotional aspects of pain. A mere mention of psychological factors can make chronic pain sufferers feel accused or blamed. I felt that way. I remember asking myself punishing and difficult questions: "Is my chronic pain my fault?" "Would I be better than I am now if I weren't so upset?" I even asked myself, "Did I want to get sick because I have problems?"

It is essential to recognize:

- Chronic pain isn't anyone's fault any more than a virus or a degenerative disc. Research shows that, with rare exceptions, chronic pain sufferers led healthy and active and psychologically sound lives before their illness.
- Anything affecting the body affects the mind. So, when doctors say "There seems to be a psychogenic component underlying your condition," it's invariably true. The downside here is that a phrase about a "psychogenic component," or the tone in which it's used, can sound blaming and dismissive. And it often is.
- You don't need high hopes in order to beat chronic pain. But you do need a modicum of hope. Without it, you're drained of the energy and focus you need to get well.

Leisure time, helpful, harmful or non-existent?

Do you have built-in leisure time? More specifically, do you have one hour a day that is yours and yours alone to do what you want – whether that's napping, walking, listening to music, taking a course, writing in a journal, being with friends or playing sports?

It is so important to have time for you in order to recover from chronic pain. When I had chronic pain, I hated statements like this. It took me for ever to get any writing done because of my pain. I couldn't help my wife. I couldn't do much for my children. I felt it would be selfish to take time for myself. After all, I was a burden. I owed so much to everyone in my life.

If you feel like this, it's understandable. The "but" is this: if you don't give yourself the time you need to recover, you'll never be in a position to "pay back" the people in your life.

• If you need a half-hour or hour walk in order to help your chronic pain, take it. Recovery takes time. If you don't take the time for whatever activities or relaxation is necessary for your wellness, it's unlikely that you can raise yourself from the deeply engraved nightmares and ruts of chronic pain.

• Are you having any fun? If you feel like kicking me for asking, take an hour a week for something, *anything*, that you thoroughly enjoy.

• Are you engaging in leisure-time activities that give you pleasure, but make your chronic pain worse? Are the gyrating motions of serving a tennis ball hurting your back? Is bowling making your knee or hip worse? Is gardening tough on your body? Only you can decide whether these pleasure/pain activities are worth it. A good rule of thumb to follow is: if you know you can make strides forward in spite of the discomfort caused by a favourite activity – and if you're following a paced fitness program like the one in this book – then you're doing good things for yourself. Otherwise, you owe it to yourself to find a new activity until you're back to making steady and regular progress.

Sex: if it was in your life before chronic pain, you need it more than ever now

If sex was a happy and important part of your life before you began suffering from chronic pain, it can only add to your pain to be deprived of it now.

- You *can* have a blissful sex life – even better than before the onset of chronic pain. About 20 per cent of the survey participants for this book mentioned that their sex lives improved when they had chronic pain. How is this possible? Because they communicated more with their partners about their sexual needs. They had to because of their physical limitations. This communication, this sharing of innermost thoughts, led to greater trust and closeness. Needless to say, trust and closeness – intimacy in other words – are the best catalysts of all to a freer and more pleasurable sex life.

- When you have chronic pain, you may have to change your mental attitude more than your physical position. Fear of hurting yourself is real and needs addressing. When chronic pain is at its worst, the positions for sexual intercourse may be limited, or they may have to change. But what if intercourse is temporarily impossible? Does this mean that your sex life has to be relegated to the past? If you're capable of sexual arousal, you're capable of having a good sex life. Use your imagination. Talk about the wishes or fantasies you've had trouble expressing. Buy a good sex guide. Generally, at a time of unceasing pain, think of what pleasure there could be in your life and try to make any adjustments you can to achieve this pleasure.

- *What about physical risks?* They can be very real, of course. A man who is on top during intercourse may find that his back arches too much and aggravates his discomfort. A woman may find the same thing. Moreover, our bodies' natural pain-inhibitors, endorphins, seem to be released during sexual activity. So, when you're feeling good sexually, you may also feel less pain during sex, but more pain afterwards. Again, the best solution is to talk openly about sex with your partner. If you are honest with each other, in spite of what may embarrass you, sex can be and will be a positive part of your life.

- *Minimizing physical risks.* As mentioned, being "on top" is usually the worst position for sex if you are in pain. Ditto being on your hands and knees. Being on your back is usually better, except if there's excessive weight on you. Being on your side is usually the best position. What can you do lying on your side? Just about anything and everything.

Turning chores into pleasant achievements

Do you know how to wash the dishes, make the bed, dust and run the vacuum in the most pain-free ways? How about cooking meals, doing the laundry, rearranging furniture and doing "spring cleaning?" And what of clearing snow, gardening, raking, washing the car, cleaning the gutters, painting, window-washing and food-shopping?

Here are tips for making each of these tasks easier and more comfortable – and turning them into successes that add a sense of accomplishment, instead of a slide into pain, to your day.

- *Washing the dishes.* Stand as close to the sink as possible. Distribute your weight unevenly – first one leg, then the other. If having your arms out in front of you begins to make your back ache, or if standing more than a few minutes makes your legs or hips hurt, take breaks. Being obsessive about finishing tasks is the number one reason for incurring pain from chores!
- *Making the bed.* The key to avoiding pain is "don't reach!" If one side of the bed is against a wall, get help in moving it away from that wall before working. Keep your back straight and knees bent when tucking in bedding.
- *Dusting.* Avoid stretching. Use a long feather-duster – or a cloth rigged up on a pole – for high and low places.
- *Vacuuming.* This is the primary indoor back-slayer! Use the lightest vacuum possible. Stand as tall as possible. As a last resort, use a lightweight cannister vacuum, instead of an upright, and vacuum when kneeling. When walking from one room to the next, pull, rather than push.
- *Cooking.* Keep shifting your weight when standing. Sit for a

change of pace when you can – for peeling, mixing and other tasks. Take a good break between gathering ingredients, preparing ingredients and cooking.

- *Doing laundry.* Carry small loads – about half of what a washing machine can hold if need be. Fold clothes on a surface above waist level.
- *Re-arranging furniture.* Be a CEO – Chief Executive Observer!
- *Spring cleaning.* Start in winter, do no more than thirty minutes a day – and enjoy spring weather lying in a hammock!
- *Clearing snow.* Here are eight tips: do a 5–10 minute set of back exercises first; use a lightweight shovel; use a shovel designed for back sufferers – one with a "U-shape" between the handle and the shovel; use an electric snow-shovel; pick up half a shovelful at a time; hire a teenager; buy tall boots and wait until the snow melts; wear ice cleats (metal or plastic grippers) on your footwear and step ever so carefully!
- *Gardening.* Kneel on a cushiony pad if it's hard to bend. Lie on your side if it's hard to kneel – clothes can be cleaned and so can you! If someone walks by, and you're embarrassed about being seen lying down, tell them you're examining the collaborative wonders of worker ants! Or, better yet, forget about what anyone thinks. Take breaks. Smell the flowers. Give yourself a luxurious bath and rest afterwards.
- *Raking.* Switch hands every few minutes. If you're right-handed, and your left hand is lower on the rake, reverse your stance and your grip. Rake no more than ten minutes a day. Or use a blower. Or let the leaves collect and call them mulch.
- *Washing the car.* Use a long-handled sponge for the top of the car and for the tires. Bend from the knees rather than reach. Consider the advantage of a really dirty car – namely, it can't get much dirtier. Alternatively, go to a car wash.
- *Cleaning the gutters.* Cover them with mesh and you won't have to clean them. Or pay someone to do it. More survey participants in this book were seriously injured cleaning gutters, patching roofs and painting exteriors than doing any other outdoor chore.
- *Painting.* Never, ever, reach above eye level to paint. Your

back will hurt – and that's that. Bend, don't reach, for low areas. Take lots of rest breaks.

Knowing when *not* to be your own expert

The wisest experts in the world know when to ask for advice and help. No single source of help, including this book, can give you all that you need to hasten and maximize your recovery.

So, when should you seek additional help? Whenever you feel you should, or have any doubts at all about your health, or feel that a new treatment is worth looking into, or find your condition deteriorating, or have questions that you can't answer yourself.

Part of any individual's wisdom is knowing what he or she doesn't know. If you're not entirely certain whether or not you should seek additional help, *seek it*!

11

The Thirteen Best Exercises
for Chronic Pain

Just a few decades ago, doing exercises to prevent and beat chronic pain was unthinkable. Moving around in general was taboo for heart patients, post-surgery patients and many other ailing people who were in desperate need of getting their bodies functioning well again. Then, President John F. Kennedy, suffering from a well-publicized back problem, called in a doctor of physical and rehabilitative medicine – Hans Kraus. Dr Kraus brought along a young colleague, Dr Willibald Nagler, now the Chief of Physiatry at New York Cornell Medical Center. Soon afterward, exercise as a therapy for back pain was officially on the map, even though it would take a few decades more for a substantial number of medical doctors to accept its value.

Do we know with absolute certainty that exercise works for chronic pain? Yes. Of course, in theory, there is nothing known definitively about chronic pain except that it wrecks lives, and that no two individuals with chronic pain have the same symptoms or respond to the same treatments in the same way. But in real life it is proven day in and day out that exercise is vital for recovery from chronic pain. Common sense tells you that if you simply lie around, and don't use your body, you'll waste away and deteriorate rapidly. In this sense, exercise is not only critical for promoting recovery, but essential to life itself.

Here are two truths you must know about the relationship between chronic pain and appropriate exercises:

1. Acute (recent-onset and temporary) pain sufferers should *not* exercise until the pain is mostly gone. Start your recovery simply by moving around as best you can, giving yourself every benefit of the doubt when your inner cues are telling you to slow down. Once you can resume non-strenuous daily functions, that is the time to start a gentle exercise program.

2. ALL of the more than 1,000 chronic pain sufferers who participated in the survey for this book found some form of exercise to be therapeutic for their overall well-being and for their chronic pain.

To summarize, then, yes, you *should* exercise for your chronic pain. At the same time, you should be ever-so careful about proceeding slowly with the right exercises. And chronic pain sufferers are the best people to tell you *which* exercises are appropriate. They are the *real experts* – the people I consulted for choosing safe and proven exercises to help chronic pain sufferers improve their lives.

There may well be other good exercises for chronic pain that are not mentioned in this chapter. But the thirteen exercises that follow – gentle and conservative stretching and strengthening routines – do work and offer a proven starting point.

Gradually improved fitness – rather than trying to get yourself in gorgeous shape for the beach – is the only major point of these exercises. Please also keep these other points in mind:

- SKIP ANY EXERCISE that feels wrong to you. If it feels wrong, it probably is. These exercises are right for *almost* everyone with chronic pain, but there are always exceptions.
- EXERCISE CAUTION. Do not exceed the recommended guidelines in this chapter.
- TAKE NO RISKS. Do no harm. Check with a qualified healthcare practitioner before you start.
- START ON A GOOD DAY. All chronic pain sufferers have relatively good days and bad days. Pain levels vary from day to day. Start the exercises in this chapter when your pain is at a minimum.

- GO SLOWLY. The slower you go, the faster you'll get to a state of lessened pain and heightened fitness. Proceed in a gentle and deliberate way. If you rush through exercises, you will entirely defeat the purpose of doing them.
- WARM UP. If your joints are stiff when you wake, and you want to start your day with exercise, you'll be better able to stretch if you take a warm (not hot) bath first or use a heating pad for several minutes. Avoid drafts. Use a heater if the room is chilly.
- EXERCISE YOUR BODY *AND* MIND. Take these exercises seriously. Get "into" them with your mind and spirit. Cast away problems, worries and concerns as much as possible. Do whatever is possible to relax before beginning. Here are some suggestions:
  * Feel free. Wear loose clothing, or if you prefer and if the room is warm enough, wear no clothing. The idea is to give your body a sense of freedom a lack of restriction so that you can "stretch out".
  * Be spiritual. If you pray, or if you have a spiritual or reflective or meditative activity that you practise, consider doing this before you exercise. A calm and positive mood invariably helps you to make the most of your exercise time.
  * Stay in rhythm. Play soothing music if you wish, but avoid music that detracts from your concentration. Try to move in ways that free up your body and increase your range of motion. Keep the beat of your internal exercise rhythms, not the beat of external music. Do not watch television while exercising. Focus on your inner self, not on external distractions.
  * Avoid "routine rigidity". If it works for you to exercise daily at the same time of the day or night, then follow this consistent routine. Most people find this works best for them. However, if adhering strictly to a routine doesn't suit your schedule, do whatever does work. If that means exercising in the morning and at night on alternate days, that's fine.
  * Exercise daily . . . or as many days of the week as possible.

Exercising should be like brushing your teeth; if you don't do it once a day, you don't feel right. On the other hand, life can interfere with the best plans to exercise daily. If this happens, don't fret about a skipped day. But do try to exercise at least five days a week.

* Forget what you know about exercise generally. Ignore whatever you've ever been told about exercise, except by a knowledgeable chronic pain practitioner. Forget "no pain, no gain." Forget "instant results." Forget "don't exercise up to three hours before bedtime." (Some people can do gentle exercises at night and sleep better for it.) Forget speed. Forget "shoulds" and "have tos." Remember: The inner cues that you feel when you start your exercises – in other words, the judgment that you and only you have about your body – are the greatest wisdom you can have about what works and what doesn't work for you.

* When you lie down for the exercises that follow, lie on a well-cushioned gym mat, or a futon, or neatly folded blankets or quilts. If you can feel the floor, or if your body hurts pressing against the surface, then switch over to lying on a firm mattress. It is critical that you lie on a comfortable surface – neither too hard nor too soft. Your body will tell you what works for you.

• SUPPORT YOUR HEAD. Place a small pillow under your head when you do stretching exercises. Never use two pillows. Avoid a very plump pillow. You want just enough padding under your neck to prevent neck discomfort.

WEEKS 1 AND 2

If you can start to do regular stretching exercises successfully, no matter how cautiously you begin, no matter how few repetitions you do at first, you are on your way to a routine that will slowly but surely do wonders to promote your recovery.

Please note that the number of repetitions recommended for you are rules of thumb *only*. If your instinct tells you to go slower, please listen to your own judgment. And never exceed recommended guidelines.

WEEKS 3 AND 4

This is the make or break time for you and exercising. It's relatively easy to *start* exercising for chronic pain. It feels like a good thing to do for yourself. Everyone approves. It's sticking with exercise that's difficult. If the exercises that you were doing before your injury or illness involved weight-lifting, by this time you might have seen gains in strength, and perhaps even in muscle definition and bulk. But this isn't the case with exercises for chronic pain. They won't make you into the Body Beautiful, and you might not see results for a month.

But be kind to yourself – KEEP GOING. You're getting there, even if you don't yet feel as if you are.

WEEK 5 ONWARD

Now you can start to add speed to your progress. Your body (and mind!) should feel more ready now. You should feel a sense of joy about the progress you're making. This is a good time for you – a time of increased gains that you've worked hard to earn. Use it well and enjoy every extra repetition you can safely do.

READY . . . SET . . . START!

Exercise 1: Breathing into relaxation and out of pain
What to do:
• Lie on your back with your knees up and your arms at your sides. (**Position 1.**)

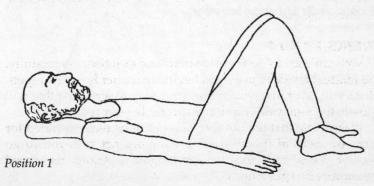

Position 1

• Take a deep breath through your stomach for a six count (about six seconds). Your belly should rise when you do this. (**Position 1a.**) To practise, put your hand on your belly when you breathe in; if your hand rises when you inhale, you're doing it right. Hold your breath for two seconds. Now exhale for a ten count (about ten seconds).

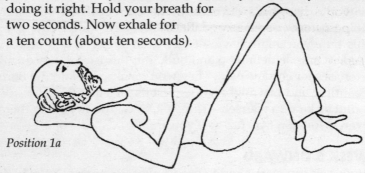

Position 1a

Number of daily repetitions, Week 1: **2**
Number of daily repetitions, Week 2: **3**
Number of daily repetitions, Week 3: **4**
Number of daily repetitions, Week 4 onward: **5**

What to think:
Think *melting*. You want to feel fluid, loose, boneless, like a rag doll. As you breathe in, picture your body filling up with relaxation. As you breathe out, imagine your body melting, flowing, relaxing into the mat or mattress you're lying on. If it helps you, say "RE" as you breathe in, and "LAX" as you breathe out.

Exercise 2: Lumbar leveller
What to do:
• Lie prone on your back with your knees up and your arms at your side. (**Position 2.**)

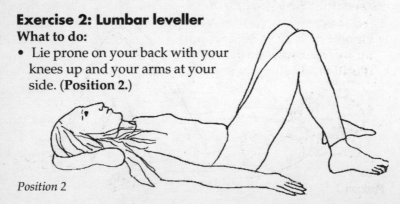

Position 2

- Use your stomach muscles to pull your abdomen in. Simultaneously, tilt your pelvis up a bit. (**Position 2a.**) Your lumbar curve or S-curve – the arched part of your lower back – should flatten toward the surface you're lying on. Hold in this flattened posture for a split second. Relax.

Position 2a

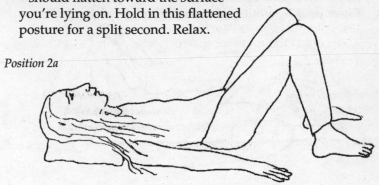

Number of daily repetitions, Week 1: **3**
Number of daily repetitions, Week 2: **4**
Number of daily repetitions, Week 3: **5**
Number of daily repetitions, Week 4 onward: **6**

What to think:
Think flexibility in the small of your back. It should feel strong but malleable – easily able to change shapes and positions, moving with ease.

Exercise 3: Single leg lifts
What to do:
- Lie on your back with your knees up and your arms at your sides. (**Position 3.**)

Position 3

- Keeping your arms at your sides, slowly lift your left knee toward your chest. Do this without straining and without trying to see how far you can raise your leg. When you reach a natural stopping point, pause for a split second, then slowly lower your leg until it's flat on the bed. (**Position 3a.**)

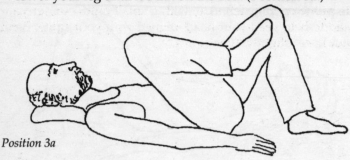

Position 3a

- Gentle wriggle your left foot, ankle and leg, for a second or two. (**Position 3b.**)

Position 3b

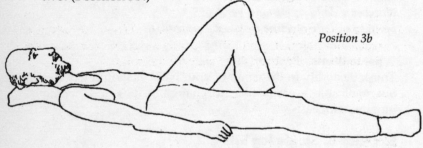

- Repeat this exercise with your right leg.

Number of daily repetitions, Week 1: **2**
Number of daily repetitions, Week 2: **3**
Number of daily repetitions, Week 3: **4**
Number of daily repetitions, Week 4 onward: **5**

What to think:
Picture your lower back loosening and stretching. When your legs are prone and stretched out on the bed, and you're wrig-

gling them one at a time, picture them uncoiling and elongating.

Exercise 4: Side leg lifts
What to do:
- Lie prone on your left side, with a small pillow under your head to help keep your head aligned with your spine. Bend your knees slightly. **(Position 4.)**

Position 4

- Slide your right knee toward your head. When you reach a resistance point, stop and drop all the weight of your knee on the mattress. **(Position 4a.)** Pause for a second.

Position 4a

- Slowly slide your leg back to the starting position. Pause when you reach it. Wriggle your right leg for a second or two.
- Repeat this exercise while lying on your right side.

Number of daily repetitions, Week 1: **2**
Number of daily repetitions, Week 2: **3**
Number of daily repetitions, Week 3: **4**
Number of daily repetitions, Week 4 onward: **5**

What to think:
While you're in this most comfortable position for lying down (lying on your side with your knees bent), focus on alternatively stretching and relaxing your legs, hips and lower back. Then envision relaxing *all* of you – body and mind.

Exercise 5: Buttock clenches

These are buttock squeezes that you do yourself – and that can do wonders for your lower back. You need your buttock muscles in good condition. We're not going to get technical about all the important muscles in the backside, but we're going to try to improve them – so that it becomes possible and comfortable for you to stand with your bottom tucked in instead of sticking out in an awkward manner.

What to do:
• Lie facing down. If you have any trouble at all with your lower back, put a modest-sized (not large or too firm) pillow under your lower abdomen. The bottom of the pillow should not be more than four inches below your navel; the top should not be higher than four inches below your nipple line. **(Position 5.)**

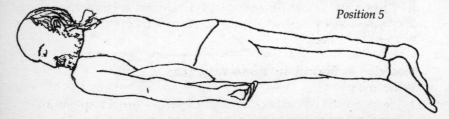

Position 5

• Squeeze your buttocks together for about five seconds. Then relax for a second. **(Position 5a.)** Years ago, an author of an exercise book wrote that you should pretend there's a coin

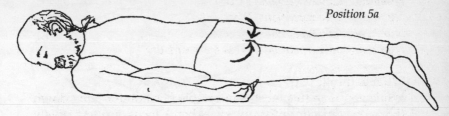

Position 5a

between your buttocks and that you're going to try and squeeze it. If this mental picture doesn't work for you, simply squeeze hard as if you were trying to keep your anus tightly shut. If this makes you giggle, create your own mental picture. To test whether you're doing the exercise correctly, place one of your hands on one of your buttocks while you're doing this exercise. As you do the exercise, your buttocks should become more taut and firm.

Number of daily repetitions, Week 1: **3**
Number of daily repetitions, Week 2: **4**
Number of daily repetitions, Week 3: **5**
Number of daily repetitions, Week 4 onward: **6,** with one more each week until you reach **10** repetitions.

What to think:
Other than thinking that this exercise is silly, and that someone watching you would have no idea which part of your body you are exercising, think of these buttock clenches as utterly essential. When you strengthen your buttock muscles, it helps you to keep your spine properly aligned and to minimize chronic pain in your lower back.

Exercise 6: Shoulder blade squeezes
What to do:
- Lie prone on your back with your knees up. Clasp your hands together behind your head. (**Position 6.**)
- Gently tighten the muscles in your upper back as if you were trying to make your shoulder blades come closer to each other. (See **Position 6a** for what should be happening if you

Position 6   *Position 6a*

were doing the exercise standing up. This drawing is for
illustrative purposes only; do not stand up to do this exercise.) Hold this muscle-tightening position for three seconds.
Relax for a second.

Number of daily repetitions, Week 1: **2**
Number of daily repetitions, Week 2: **3**
Number of daily repetitions, Week 3: **4**
Number of daily repetitions, Week 4 onward: **5**

What to think:
The upper back is rarely discussed in books. It is sadly
neglected, midway between more celebrated parts, hard at

work in the traffic between your brain and the rest of you. So, when you do the squeezing part of this exercise, feel and picture the labyrinth of muscles and other soft tissue in this powerful yet troublesome area. When you stop squeezing, really let go. Let everything in your upper back unwind.

Exercise 7: Double leg raise
What to do:
- Lie on your back with your knees up and your arms at your side. (**Position 7.**)

Position 7

- Clasp your hands together just below your knees. (**Position 7a.**)

Position 7a

- Exhaling, pull your legs slowly and gently toward your chest. (**Position 7b.**)

Position 7b

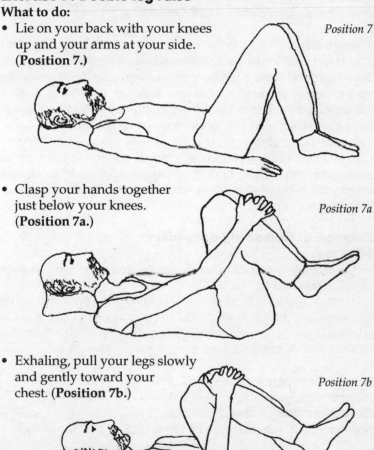

- When you get to the point of light resistance, hold it there for five seconds, keeping slight pressure toward your chest.
- Return your legs slowly to the starting position.

Number of daily repetitions, Week 1: **3**
Number of daily repetitions, Week 2: **4**
Number of daily repetitions, Week 3: **5**
Number of daily repetitions, Week 4 onward: **6**

What to think:
You'll feel your lower back stretch when you do these exercises. You might feel some stretching in your legs and hips as well. As you exercise, picture your entire torso in a flowing state – rubbery, loose, elastic. Do *not* anticipate a point of resistance. Start the stretch as if you could move through time and space. Let your body give you cues about how far you can stretch. (Note: if you're in a particularly painful state, and not up to exercising, you might find it of pain-easing value to simply clasp your hands just below your knees, and hold in this position for a minute or so.

Exercise 8: Hamstring extenders
What to do:
- Lie on your back with your knees up and your arms at your side. **(Position 8.)**

Position 8

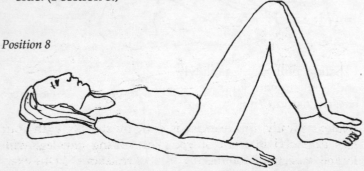

- Raise your left knee about six inches toward your chest. **(Position 8a.)** Extend your foot toward the ceiling, then

Position 8a

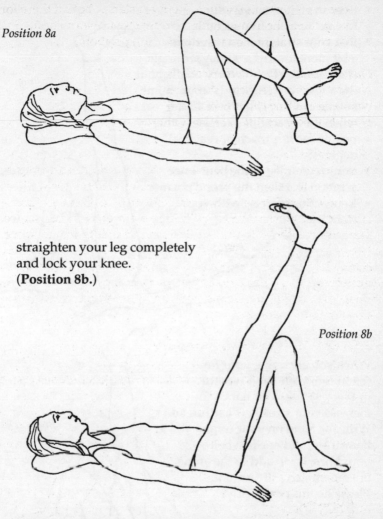

straighten your leg completely
and lock your knee.
(**Position 8b.**)

Position 8b

(Note: typically, this exercise is done by starting with your legs extended in front of you, and raising one leg, with locked knee, until you reach a point of resistance. In the exercise above, we add the extra step of raising your leg from a bent-knee position. This is safer for you. Lifting one or both legs from a leg-prone position can injure your lower back.)

- Ever so gently, move your leg toward you, for five seconds, so that your straightened leg moves a bit more toward a 90-degree angle. (**Position 8c.**) Don't worry at all about the angle your leg winds up in. Some people can barely get past 45 degrees when they start this exercise. Other people can approach or reach 90 degrees.
- Return your leg to the bent-knee position and then the prone position.
- Repeat this exercise with your right leg.

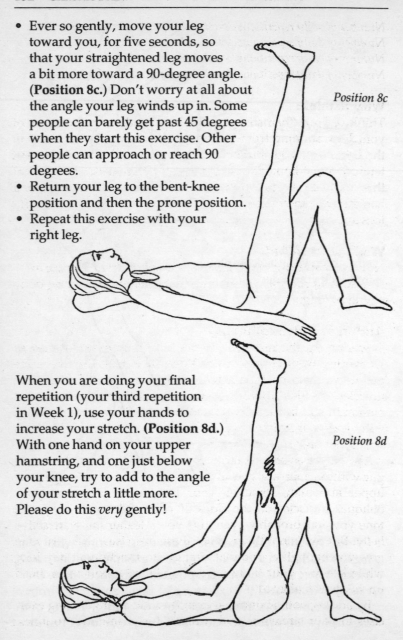

Position 8c

When you are doing your final repetition (your third repetition in Week 1), use your hands to increase your stretch. (**Position 8d.**) With one hand on your upper hamstring, and one just below your knee, try to add to the angle of your stretch a little more. Please do this *very* gently!

Position 8d

Number of daily repetitions, Week 1: **3**
Number of daily repetitions, Week 2: **4**
Number of daily repetitions, Week 3: **5**
Number of daily repetitions, Week 4 onward: **6**

What to think:
Think of your "hamstring" – the long tendons in the backs of your legs, running from just above the backs of your knees to the bottom of your buttocks. These extraordinarily important tendons must be kept both strong and stretched. The point of this exercise is to stretch them. Shortened or tightened hamstrings can create a mess of body aches, including painful legs and back.

WEEK 4 ONWARD
Now is the time for you to add two kinds of strengthening exercises to your routine: abdominal strengthening and upper-body strengthening.

Abdominal strengthening
Powering up the muscles in your gut is an essential part of recovering from chronic pain. While it is true that there are people with no back pain who don't have strong abdominal muscles, it's also true that almost all of the recovered chronic pain sufferers in the survey for this book felt better generally, with less pain, after they did a few weeks of abdominal-strengthening exercises.

The exercises shown here are designed to strengthen your gut without injuring you in the process. Some work on your upper abdomen, some on your lower gut, others on your obliques (muscles on the sides of your abdomen). They will tone you and probably even give you a leaner more attractive belly. But that's not the point of these exercises. Our goal is to give you enough abdominal strength to function all day long while keeping your body properly aligned – bottom in, head up, body well aligned.

By adding both abdominal exercises and strengthening exercises to your stretching and walking (or swimming) routines, you'll feel better overall, be able to prevent and ease chronic pain and be in better shape than most people who have never experienced chronic pain.

Exercise 9: Head up (upper abs)

- Lie on your back with your knees up. Put your hands, palms up, on the back of your head. (**Position 9.**) You'll know you're in the right position when your fingertips graze your pillow.

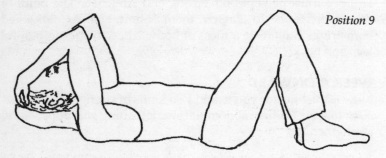

Position 9

- Using your arms as levers, lift your head slowly until you can see your navel. (**Position 9a.**) Move your head slowly back to the pillow. Relax.

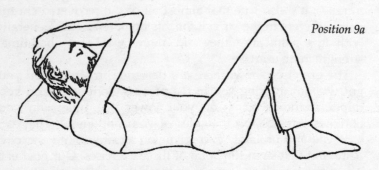

Position 9a

Number of daily repetitions, Week 1: **3**
Number of daily repetitions, Week 2: **4**
Number of daily repetitions, Week 3: **5**
Number of daily repetitions, Week 4 onward: **7**

For more advanced conditioning, work your way up to **15** repetitions by adding one more each week.

Exercise 10: Knees to chest (upper abs)

- Lie on your back with your knees up and your hands clasped around your knees. (**Position 10.**)

Position 10

- Simultaneously pull your knees toward your chest and move your head toward your knees. (**Position 10a.**) Do this slowly for a five-count.

Position 10u

Number of daily repetitions, Week 1: **3**
Number of daily repetitions, Week 2: **4**
Number of daily repetitions, Week 3: **5**
Number of daily repetitions, Week 4 onward: **7**

For more advanced conditioning, work your way up to **15** repetitions by adding one more each week.

Exercise 11: Head to opposite knee (lower abs and obliques)

- Lie on your back with your right ankle propped up just below your left knee. (**Position 11.**)

Position 11

- Place your left hand, palm up, behind your head. (**Position 11a.**) Guiding your head with your left hand, move your head toward your right knee. (**Position 11b.**) Relax.
- Repeat with your left ankle propped up just below your right knee.

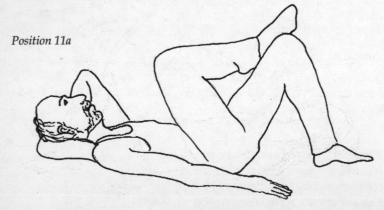

Position 11a

Position 11b

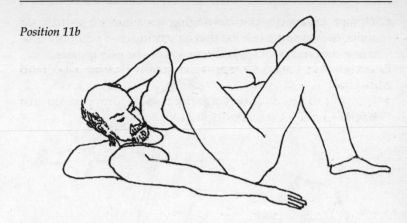

Number of daily repetitions, Week 1: **3**
Number of daily repetitions, Week 2: **4**
Number of daily repetitions, Week 3: **5**
Number of daily repetitions, Week 4 onward: **7**

For more advanced conditioning, work your way up to **15** repetitions by adding one more each week.

Exercise 12: Knees to chest (Upper abs)
- Lie on your back with your knees up and your arms at your side. **(Position 12.)**

Position 12

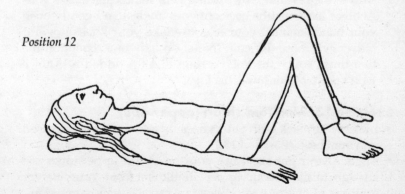

- Tighten your gut and slowly bring your knees toward your chest. **(Position 12a.)** Note that as you reach a point of resistance, the effort required of your lower abs gets greater.

Position 12a

Number of daily repetitions, Week 1: **3**
Number of daily repetitions, Week 2: **4**
Number of daily repetitions, Week 3: **5**
Number of daily repetitions, Week 4 onward: **7**

For more advanced conditioning:
1. Work your way up to **15** repetitions by adding one more each week.
2. Add to the resistance by placing your hands just above your Achilles tendons (the backs of your ankles) and gently push your hands against your legs to make your knees-upward movement more difficult. (Note: do only one repetition the first time. You want to be certain that the added resistance won't bother your lower back.)

Exercise 13: Modified sit up (upper abs)
- Lie on your back with your knees up and your arms crossed on your chest. **(Position 13.)**
- Tighten your gut and raise your head and upper torso just enough to clear your upper shoulders from your mat or mattress. **(Position 13a.)** When you can see your navel, stop.

Position 13

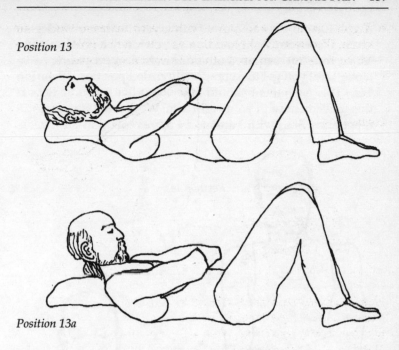

Position 13a

Number of daily repetitions, Week 1: **3**
Number of daily repetitions, Week 2: **4**
Number of daily repetitions, Week 3: **5**
Number of daily repetitions, Week 4 onward: **7**

For more advanced conditioning, work your way up to **15** repetitions by adding one more rep each week.

Strengthening exercises

If you're thinking, "but I don't have time to do more exercises," don't worry because the exercises that follow take no time at all because you do them while you walk or while you are stationary. They don't represent a systematic strengthening programme, but rather a fun way to add power to your upper body while walking. The survey participants who suggested these exercises all had the same response to them: "They take no time and they make me stronger."

- *Biceps.* Extend your left arm, with elbow bent, at a 90-degree angle. Place your right hand on your left wrist. (**Position 14.**) Move your left arm up, with your right arm providing resistance, until you get to a completely curled position. (**Position 14a.**) This movement should take about five seconds. Repeat this movement with your right arm. Work your way up to **10** repetitions. Start with **3** and add **1** more repetition each week.

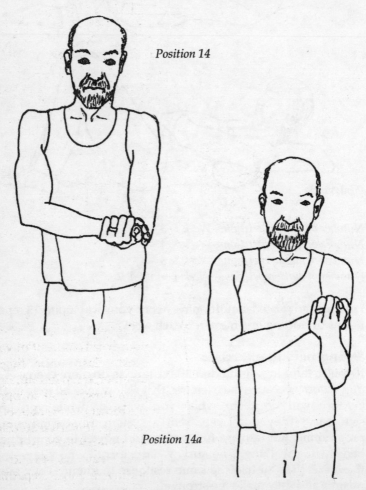

Position 14

Position 14a

- *Pecs.* Extend your hands in front of your chest and press your palms together for about five seconds. **(Position 15.)** Start with **3** repetitions and work your way up to **10** by adding **1** more repetition every week.

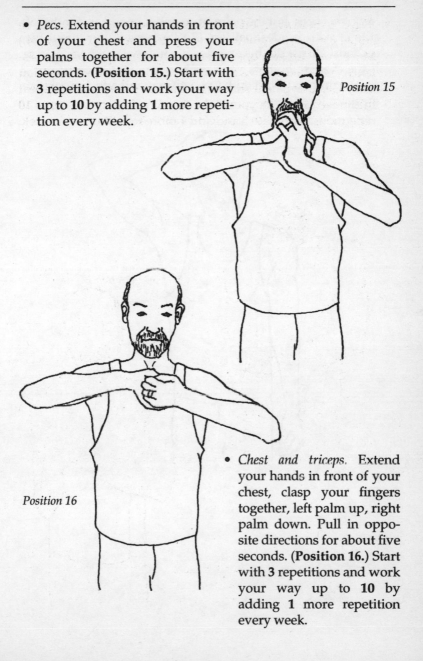

Position 15

Position 16

- *Chest and triceps.* Extend your hands in front of your chest, clasp your fingers together, left palm up, right palm down. Pull in opposite directions for about five seconds. **(Position 16.)** Start with **3** repetitions and work your way up to **10** by adding **1** more repetition every week.

- *Neck and biceps.* Put the palm of your left hand against the left side of your head. (**Position 17.**) Push *gently* for about five seconds. Do *not* do this exercise if you have any neck pain or if the exercise bothers your neck in any way. Repeat using your right hand. Start with **2** repetitions and add **1** more each week for three weeks.

Position 17

- *Neck, shoulders and upper back.* Clasp your hands behind your head. **(Position 18.)** Keeping your head straight, pull gently with your hands against your head. This resistance will add tone to your neck muscles as well as to your shoulders and upper back. Again, if you have any neck pain, skip this exercise.

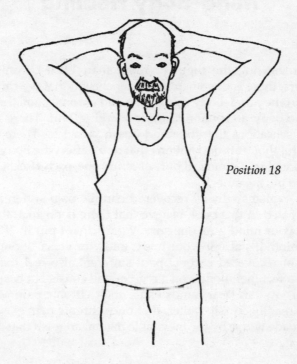

Position 18

12

Mind–Body Healing

After reviewing the input of more than 1,000 chronic pain sufferers, there is one unanimous conclusion that we can come to about the mind–body connection and chronic pain: the mind and the body are one indivisible working unit. There are no bodily sensations that the mind doesn't react to. There are no powerful thoughts or emotions that don't affect the body. Body and mind, for all practical purposes, are one; each affects, and is affected by, the other.

This explains why *all* recovered chronic pain sufferers who participated in this book believe that there is no such thing as "all in your mind". As one survey participant put it, "If it's in your mind, it's also in your body, and vice versa." Some two-thirds of recovered chronic pain sufferers also feel that their minds affect their bodies on a regular and consistent basis. This isn't to say that their minds cause their chronic pain and can just as readily cure it; rather, that once chronic pain exists, it is often made worse by the inevitable mental anguish that accompanies it.

WHAT THIS CHAPTER WILL AND WON'T DO FOR YOU

There are hundreds of books in print that focus on specific self-healing therapies that promote mind–body health. This book isn't one of them. Instead, this book covers general self-healing approaches that recovered chronic pain sufferers can use with success. Why this focus on general approaches rather than on specific techniques? Because, in the survey for this book, no two people agreed on the precise methodology and proven healing power of much-touted techniques such as guided imagery, yoga as a spiritual discipline, meditation or self-hypnosis. These techniques were mentioned, but the number of frustrations and failures associated with the techniques were greater than the number of successes.

In the words of one survey participant: "I'd like to spend the rest of my life learning from the great masters the many different techniques that enable the mind to heal the body. But, when I was in constant and dire pain, I had neither the time nor the energy to acquire this mastery.

"Instead, I focused on general approaches. When I recovered from chronic pain, I went on to other things, and never did learn these specific mind–body disciplines. I did, however, become aware of ways of looking at my life to help bring about mind–body well-being."

MIND–BODY PERSPECTIVES THAT CAN LEAD TO IMMEDIATE HEALING OUTCOMES

Before we look at seven mind–body approaches to healing chronic pain, let's briefly address two basic questions that keep arising:

1. Is there proof that the mind–body connection exists for bringing about and maintaining good health?
2. Does the mind–body connection have any practical value for chronic pain sufferers?

The mind–body connection is real. Infants who aren't stroked and cuddled have a high mortality rate. Adults suffering intense grief – from the loss of a loved one or from the break-up of a marriage, for example – have a higher death rate. Older people who have loving pets in their lives get sick less often and live longer. On the other hand, no matter how positive we are and no matter how well we live, we remain mortal. So, the mind–body connection has its limitations as well as its miracles. Mostly, it has mysteries, unknowns and infinite potential.

Here are some of the kinds of mind–body connections that worked for the recovered chronic pain sufferers who participated in this book's research. They are simple and constitute approaches to living and believing that anyone can use straightaway.

Mind–Body Approach 1: Letting go of blame

In my dialogue with more than 1,000 recovered chronic pain sufferers, the idea of blaming oneself for having chronic pain was always a factor. The main reason for the high incidence of self-blame among this group is that chronic pain disease isn't taken seriously by the healthcare professions. Indeed, your chances of getting the same diagnosis for chronic pain from different practitioners are minimal. There is no certified healthcare specialty for chronic pain, and there is virtually no chronic pain management training in medical schools or in internships. The diagnosis most often heard from a healthcare profession that doesn't yet take chronic pain seriously? "There's nothing really wrong with you."

Nothing could be worse for the chronic pain sufferer than this finger-pointing. If no one can explain what's wrong with us, or if no one can agree about our diagnosis and prognosis, then maybe we want to be sick with pain. Maybe we're psychologically a lot sicker than we think. Maybe it's our tension at work or our troubled marriage. Maybe we're to blame for our chronic pain.

Please put that kind of thinking out of your mind. You're no more responsible for your chronic pain than you would be for your ulcer (no, it's not stress-caused), your heart disease or your mental illness. However, you are responsible for trying to stop allocating blame to yourself. This is easier said than done, I know, but try to believe in and live the following blame-beaters on a daily basis:

- **Tell yourself**: I suffer from a widespread medical epidemic. Millions of others have the same affliction. They didn't bring it on. I didn't bring it on.
- **Tell yourself:** To the extent that I am in a negative mood because of my painful condition, and to the extent that my troubled state *may* add to my physical pain, I'll be open to

looking honestly at this and seeking counseling if it's needed.

- **Tell yourself**: If I'm blaming healthcare practitioners for my chronic pain condition, I will try to drop this blaming attitude, even if there are good reasons to assign this blame. I accept that I need to move forward, and that blaming others is getting me nowhere.

Mind–Body Approach 2: Finding the value of your illness and making it a part of your recovery

I asked 1,000 chronic pain sufferers whether their years of chronic pain had given them any new and worthwhile perspectives about their lives, their relationships, their priorities, their sense of what life was for. In short, I asked them whether they had gotten any value out of their illness, no matter how great their losses had been. All answered yes.

Then I asked the following question to those same sufferers: "If you could go back and wipe out the years you spent in chronic pain, would you?" Half of the respondents said they wouldn't! They felt they got so much more out of life now because of what they had learned about life while in chronic pain, they wouldn't want to give up those new perspectives.

I spent four years in bed and four more years making it back to a full recovery. That's eight years out of my life as an active person. Wouldn't I want those years back if I had the power to get them back? Surprisingly, no. Those years, as horrific as they were, with my life hanging in the balance, gave me a truer sense of myself, as nothing else could have done. For example, I have love now, because the risk of being seen and being vulnerable and being loved is a risk I'm willing to take. I value every day more. I count my blessings more. I try to think of how I might do more for others. I understand myself better. I have fewer secrets, from myself and from others. When I was sick, I had so little to lose, I was so close to death, that I found the most essential truths about myself, and as a result, have the new-found ability to live my life more fully now.

What is the value of *your* illness? What have you learned that you can take with you into your recovery. Consider this idea, as expressed by one survey participant for this book: "Only those who have truly suffered can truly appreciate this miracle of life." Search for the value in your illness and move forward into life with it.

Mind–Body Approach 3: Considering the placebo effect

I asked online survey participants: "Can you think of anything – preferably something that you've never seen in a book – that you think might help chronic pain sufferers?" The answer that came up most was the placebo effect – a healing effect from a treatment that has no known medical value. The number of replies wasn't large enough to claim scientific validity for it, but it's a thought-provoking idea.

One survey respondent put it this way: "I'll never know if the treatment I took worked – maybe it was just the power of suggestion – but I started to get well." Treatments that can elicit a placebo effect can be anything at all – a muscle relaxant, a visit to a faith healer, Vitamin C, Vitamin E, a macrobiotic diet, electric stimulation , to name a few. They all have in common the fact that survey participants didn't know themselves whether it was the treatment that worked, or whether it was the placebo effect.

Is there an approach to healing yourself that you think might work, that you've been reluctant to try? If so, and if you know with absolute certainty that you can't do yourself any harm, and you've consulted first with a qualified healthcare practitioner, and you know that you won't be overly disappointed if the approach doesn't work, my suggestion is to give this healing approach a try and give yourself over to believing as strongly as you can that it will work. The reality is that the *expectation* of getting well can make us well about one in three times for a wide range of ailments. You could believe in the placebo effect on the grounds that you have nothing to lose.

Mind–Body Approach 4: Two myths that destroy self-healing

Beware of these two wellness-defeating myths:

1. "There must be someone out there who can help you." This statement, no matter how well meant, can be a trap – one that leaves you feeling that if you make the rounds of practitioners long enough, someone is going to have the answer for you.

The trap here is that it leaves *you* out of the healing equation. It minimizes the value of your belief in yourself. Remember: you are the ultimate expert about your chronic pain symptoms and, at best, a highly competent practitioner can only help you, not cure you. If you think that you should consult with additional healthcare practitioners, read chapter 14, "Healthcare Practitioners: Who to See, Who to Avoid" first.

2. "There must be a treatment that works." A single treatment that cures chronic pain is a rare exception. There is seldom a "magic bullet" for chronic pain disease, unlike many diseases that do have a single cure. Even if a single drug therapy, for example, got rid of your chronic pain, there might well be a need for other treatments, ranging from physical therapy to occupational therapy to psychotherapy, to restore your life to fullness after years of incapacitation.

Mind–Body Approach 5: Focusing more on treatment than diagnosis

It is a maxim in Western medicine that there can be no treatment without a diagnosis. Chronic pain turns this common wisdom on its ear. Chronic pain is a "default diagnosis". There is no specific medical test for it. If all other medical tests fail to turn up a specific physical cause for your constant and long-term pain, then chronic pain is your diagnosis by default, whether your healthcare practitioner calls it that or not.

My point is a simple one: you can recover from chronic pain

whether or not you have a diagnosis of chronic pain. The key is to be utterly painstaking in insisting that every other medical ailment is ruled out. Push, complain, assert yourself, don't take no for an answer, especially in a day and age when doctors are sometimes reluctant to order large numbers of tests.

Once you have a diagnosis of chronic pain – whether by the skilled reasoning of a wise practitioner or simply by default – you have to move on to recovery. And you have to give up the idea of getting a specific diagnosis. To insist on a diagnosis that is not yet a standard one in medicine is to delay the hope for recovery and to put off devising a well-thought-out treatment plan. There *is* hope without a specific diagnosis. There *is* recovery without a specific diagnosis. In this book, more than 900 out of 1,000 recovered pain sufferers made it back to life without a specific diagnosis of chronic pain.

Mind–Body Approach 6: It isn't your body that has to get well; it's all of you

There is no chronic pain without mental pain. No one, except the severely mentally ill, has ever had debilitating pain for three months or three years or three decades without their mind being affected. It's upsetting to have the flu for one week. It's completely upsetting to your mind and body to spend weeks in bed with a broken limb.

The mental pain that invariably accompanies chronic pain isn't your fault. Our minds and our bodies are one. If you did *not* feel at all distressed that chronic pain was limiting your life, you would quite likely have a serious mental illness requiring treatment.

The lesson to learn here is that you must have hope in your life, no matter how slim and tenuous, in order to risk recovery. What is the risk? If you go all out to get well, you might not get the results you want and this is a frightening possibility.

Mind–Body Approach 7: Using anger to fight back

Anger can be the dangerous undertow of chronic pain, pulling us downward with despair and self-blame. Alternatively, anger can be the new wave of energy that gets us safely to a harbor of wellness.

Try to put your anger to work *for* you, not against you.

- Use it as a focus to believe in yourself and to stick with a good recovery plan.
- Use it to push aside the failures of the past and to believe in the future.
- Use it to avoid the pitfalls of living with chronic pain: doing too much one day and spending the next few days laid up; listening to well-meant but misleading advice about what you should do for your chronic pain; and buying the myth that chronic pain is somehow your fault.
- Use it to push determinedly toward a better life.

13

How to Choose a Healthcare Practitioner

To better understand the one essential truth you must grasp in order to select a good healthcare partner for chronic pain, let's try a short exercise in deductive reasoning.

The syllogism goes like this: "Doctors are people. Some people are insightful, brilliant *and* caring. Therefore, some doctors are insightful, brilliant *and* caring." You want to choose one of *these* doctors, of course. The question is: how do you find one? No single practitioner you will find is likely to be brilliant about all phases of chronic pain management. The training that would lead to this kind of all-round expertise doesn't exist today in medical schools. But there are many physicians and other kinds of healthcare practitioners who are good and compassionate healers, who are aware of their limitations, and who also know when to refer you, and where.

The point of this chapter is to help you find these best-possible practitioners, and not incidentally, dodge those who are more likely than not to give you an even greater pain in the wherever.

A SHORT SHORT STORY ABOUT A LONG-TERM MIRACLE OF HEALING

When I turned forty, I had the world turning nicely in my direction. I had my own business. My then-wife and I were expecting our first child. I was training for marathons, lifting weights and playing a lot of tennis.

Then, within a span of six months, my life careened into a world of pain. I developed a painful right Achilles tendon, an inability to move my right ankle from side to side, an inability to step forward on my right foot, fasiculations (rapid, visibly fluttering muscle jerking) throughout my body, severe muscle cramping everywhere there were muscles, aching in my legs and back and, finally, a state of incapacitation. I could barely get out of bed. I couldn't bathe myself. I was an invalid. I felt as if my life was over.

I started making the rounds of healthcare practitioners. Just getting there, and being examined, was an ordeal that often made me feel worse. Over three years, I saw thirteen practitioners. These included an internist, orthopedist, neurologist, podiatrist, physical therapist, doctor of Chinese medicine, shiatsu therapist, acupuncturist, osteopath, chiropractor, homeopathic doctor and faith healer. None of them helped me substantially.

The fourteenth doctor, however, changed my life. He may well have saved my life. John J. Halperin, now chairman of the department of neurology at North Shore University Hospital, is a brilliant doctor. But it wasn't his brilliance that mattered most to me. Dr Halperin wasn't put off by the thick folder that lay in front of him during my initial visit. He was challenged. He took an interest. He asked questions and listened for a full hour. A month later, the battery of tests he had ordered came back. I went to see him about the results. Dr Halperin walked into the patients' waiting area to get me. As we made our way slowly toward his office, he stopped and said: "I don't know exactly what's wrong with you, Art. It frustrates me not to know. In neurology, we often don't know as much as we would like. My feeling is that your condition is five to ten years ahead of what medical science knows." I felt saddened. Dr Halperin went on: "But, Art, I'll do everything I can to work with you and to help you." In more than three years, no one had ever spoken those words to me. Tears suddenly came to my eyes and I couldn't say anything for a few seconds. "Thank you," was all I finally could say. I felt hope again. I felt the euphoric rush of life's good possibilities. After a tormenting, doubt-filled journey of pain and isolation, I felt I could make it back to wellness because a doctor took me seriously, and wanted to do everything he could possibly do to help.

Amazing, isn't it? This power of kindness. The healing miracles that can transcend inexplicable ailments and transform our beings when we feel understood and supported! We can give the strength for recovery to another person simply by bestowing on them our wholehearted concern. The word "caring" has been reduced today to clichés and advertising slogans. But the life force that caring generates should never be underestimated. Its power is worlds beyond a touchy-feely phrase or a new-age mantra. It is powerful medicine and essential to the art of great doctoring. It underlies the human force that can lift us to new levels. Caring is essential to life. No one, not one of us, does as well as we might without another human being believing in us. This isn't one man's opinion about the role of caring in working with chronic pain sufferers. Most of this book's survey participants have a similar story to tell.

So, the first rule for choosing a doctor is a simple one: he or she must be caring and supportive, both personally and professionally. This isn't a given, and it isn't easy – like writing a prescription. It takes time to get to know a patient well, and it takes humility to admit to *not* having all the answers.

WHY FAMOUS DOCTORS ARE USUALLY NOT GOOD BETS

I had excellent contacts for healthcare when I was ill. My former wife was a science writer for the *New York Times*. I knew a number of prominent physicians and was able to move to the front of the line in getting appointments. With few exceptions, the doctors I saw were heads of departments and familiar figures in the media.

Dr Lewis "Bud" Rowland, of Columbia-Presbyterian Hospital, was one of these doctors. To the public, he is perhaps best known for treating Mohammad Ali's Parkinson's disease. When I saw Dr Rowland, he was widely considered to be the doyen of neurologists, the brightest light of them all. Saying his name to others in his specialty elicited awe and high praise. But, the bright light, in this case, grew dim and negative for a chronic pain sufferer. Dr Rowland had one comment during his examination: "You look in good shape; how much do you exercise every day?" I weighed 112 pounds at the time, down from the 140 I weighed before my three years of being laid up. We sat down to talk after a routine five-minute examination. Dr Rowland commented again that I seemed in good physical condition and added that my tests showed nothing wrong with me. He then said: "It never fails. Every Friday, I see someone like you. They tell me about their symptoms, and I tell them there's nothing wrong with them. I think there is a psychogenic component underlying your condition and suggest that you consider treatment in that area." The fee for the ten minutes with Dr Rowland, some fifteen years ago, was $400. The emotional price I paid for being labelled as a typical Friday patient was greater than that.

I was seeing a psychotherapist at the time. The sessions were invaluable in helping me deal with the depression and fears caused by my incapacitation. *Every* illness and incapacitation has a psychological component, perhaps most especially chronic pain. But the impact on me of a renowned neurologist categorizing three years of incapacitation as "nothing wrong" was disheartening. More than that, it led to weeks of my agonizing over whether I had perhaps unwittingly caused or perpetuated my chronic pain, and could walk away from it if I cared to.

Another of this book's survey participants went to see the chairman of orthopedics at one of the most famous teaching hospitals in the USA. He was carried in on a stretcher, after two years of being bedridden. The doctor told him he had some spinal arthritis (normal for his age) and prescribed "buffered acetylsalicylic acid" – two tablets four times a day for two weeks. "Buffered aspirin" asked the patient incredulously? The doctor nodded yes. "And if I'm not better in two weeks?" asked the patient, now in tears. "Get dressed please", said the doctor, as he left the room.

The majority of this book's 200 survey participants who noted that they saw eminent physicians considered these doctors to be unhelpful, dismissive and unwilling to take seriously any condition that didn't show up on medical tests. These media-renowned doctors were less willing to "not know" and work with the mysteries of chronic pain. As one survey participant put it: "It takes time away from patients for a doctor to become well known. The most brilliant medical mind in the world can look silly dealing with the peculiarities of each different case of chronic pain. Famous doctors have little patience for looking foolish."

PROS AND CONS OF SPECIALISTS

"Maybe you should see a specialist," is a sentiment heard by virtually everyone who has ever suffered unexplained pain for more than a few days. Maybe, but *which* specialist? And *is* there a specialist for chronic pain?

There is no board-certified specialty in chronic pain management. But, there are specialists who tend to deal in particular kinds of treatments and evaluations regarding chronic pain.

For example, *anaesthesiologists* specialize in the latest pain-killing techniques – using laser technology, thermal heat, electrical currents, delivery of painkillers to specific areas of the body and other methods.

Neurologists treat diseases that affect nerves and muscles.

Orthopedists deal with ailments and diseases affecting the musculoskeletal system.

Physiatrists help to restore bodily movement and function.

Rheumatologists concentrate on arthritic conditions.

Internists probe your overall internal functioning to see if it reveals a basis for pain.

Urologists work with urino-genital functions.

Proctologists start from the bottom up in trying to determine the origin of chronic pain.

Perhaps more to the point, there is a relatively new pain specialty called *algology*. Its members consist mostly of the specialties listed above. Algology is not yet a board-certified specialty, and it lacks widely accepted models for treating chronic pain. What algologists have in common is a strong interest in treating pain; that interest alone can have great value for the chronic pain sufferer.

Please also read chapters 14 and 15 for details about the relative efficacy of different kinds of practitioners and treatments.

THE CRITICAL ROLE OF A REFERRING PRACTITIONER

For most major diseases that threaten the quality or duration of our lives, primary-care practitioners are our gateway to health. They spot our problem – hopefully, before it gets out of hand. They send us to specialists when necessary. They give us or get us the help we need. At least that's the way it's supposed to work.

In practice, for chronic pain sufferers, it almost never works like this. This reality goes a long way to explain why chronic pain has reached epidemic proportions, why it is not diminishing and why there is no overall breakthrough in sight at the moment.

Primary care doctors are, for the most part, however unintentionally, misrepresenting themselves to the general public in terms of their qualifications for helping chronic pain sufferers. Study after study in areas like back pain show these practitioners to be inadequate in their ability to provide or refer a road to recovery. In this book's survey, the lowest rating of all was given to the doctor we see the most for what ails us. After colds, chronic pain is the most popular reason for seeing our primary care practitioner. Too often, for the chronic pain sufferer, this doctor we most rely on marks the beginning of the end of hope.

However, this does not mean that primary care physicians should shoulder the lion's share of blame for the deplorable status of treatments for chronic pain. The blame is equally distributed among the medical profession, other healthcare professions and the schools and the institutes that train them. If a shoemaker knew as little about shoes as the average doctor knows about pain, we'd be a barefoot society. The average medical doctor has less than three hours of training in chronic pain management, and is as ill-prepared to treat chronic pain as a car mechanic who doesn't know how an engine works.

Does this mean that you should despair of finding an all-round, co-ordinating physician for your chronic pain woes? No. There are specialties, *neurology*, for example, where medical mysteries are as routine as the known and curable. This explains why neurologists are rated in this book as the best overall "co-ordinators" for chronic pain. Physiatrists (doctors of physical and rehabilitative medicine) are also rated highly. They, too, are accustomed to working with difficult and often inexplicable physiological symptoms.

HOW TO KNOW IF YOU HAVE A GOOD CO-ORDINATING PRACTITIONER

If you can check off all of the criteria below, you have yourself a good co-ordinating practitioner for chronic pain. By "co-ordinating," I mean someone who can either provide you with all the input or treatment you need – or can refer you to the additional specialized help you might need. In theory, no single medical discipline can provide the full range of help needed for chronic pain – from acupuncture to nerve blocks, massage to medication. Hence the emphasis here on "co-ordinating".

If you can answer yes to at least six of the eight criteria below, you can be reasonably certain that you're receiving a high level of professional help.

1. Understanding that chronic pain *is* a disease in itself, not the absence of a diagnosis.
2. Understanding that it usually takes a multi-faceted approach to resolve chronic pain illness. For example, even if a particular medication alleviates your symptoms, you may still want to look into long-term ways to keep pain at bay without medication. You may also need occupational therapy if you've been out of work for years, or if your work is physically demanding. In addition, you may need help repairing and restoring relationships strained or lost through your long illness, starting with your relationship with yourself! There is no single model treatment that cures chronic pain. There are books and practitioners that claim a single

magic-bullet cure such as exercise, stress reduction, a changed attitude and the like – but all these are bogus claims.

3. Empathy and compassion for what it means to have chronic pain. To quote the astute authors of the guide for professionals, *Handbook of Pain Management*, "The art of comfort is as important as the advancements of science."

4. Humility. It is difficult, but critically important, for a practitioner to keep in mind what he or she doesn't know. In the widely read book, *Mastering Pain*, by Richard Sternback, MD, the author ignores these three key words – "I don't know." Here's one example from his book:

> These, then, are the major possibilities for diagnosis if there is no medical disease found to underlie the symptoms of [chronic] pain: the pain can be due to a stress reaction – somatization; it can be a false complaint – malingering; or it can be due to unconscious mental mechanisms – psychogenic.

5. Willingness to be a partner in tackling chronic pain, not a one-way omniscient dispenser of knowledge and information. Your practitioner has to respect your judgement about what can help and what cannot, and to be willing and able to learn from you. This is especially important because traditional medical testing tells us little if anything about the symptoms of, and possible treatments for, chronic pain. Your individualized chronic pain cannot be treated without your ability to be a teacher as well as a student and a patient.

For you, the patient, this implies a need to be "co-responsible." You can neither want, nor expect, all of the answers to come from your practitioner. Your role must be an active one. You must feel as responsible for your treatment as you want your practitioner to feel. A "cure-me" attitude is bound to fail; a "work-with-me" attitude is more likely to succeed and is appreciated by any true professional working with chronic pain.

6. Ability to be motivating. All chronic illnesses can be devastating, if not fatal, by virtue of their duration alone. This isn't an obvious point for anyone who hasn't experienced long-

term illness. Most people are used to getting well from a flu or a sprain; their vision is one of relatively fast and inevitable healing. Indeed, we almost always *do* get well from flus and sprains. Not so with chronic illnesses. The very word "chronic" is unnerving. Perhaps "non-acute" would be a better phrase. This isn't about words, but about mind-set. How optimistic can anyone be with a diagnosis that implies endless pain? Against this backdrop, it's enormously helpful to have a highly motivating healthcare practitioner working with us. When you hit a bump in your progress, it's helpful to be reminded how far you've come. If a new kind of pain crops up – a fairly common occurrence among chronic pain sufferers – encouragement is vital medicine.

7. Openness to alternative thinking and treatments. Generally, the more tools a healthcare practitioner can employ to help patients overcome pain, the better the odds of success. Traditional thinking does the job when mainstream approaches work. But when you're dealing with a complex and mysterious disease like chronic pain, "traditional" can be synonymous with "limited". If a healthcare practitioner has a healthy respect for different ways of thinking, you have a better chance of finding a healthcare arsenal that helps you win the war. This doesn't mean that *anything* is worth trying, or that a healthy skepticism isn't needed. But, for example, if a Western-trained medical doctor can't consider a range of treatments – acupuncture, natural supplements, massage, homeopathy, psychotherapy and paced exercise, for example – you probably need someone more flexible to assist your recovery.

8. A willingness to make time for the chronic pain sufferer. It is a rare doctor these days who has the time to deal with chronic pain. Discusson takes longer than medical testing, but dialogue about chronic pain between doctor and patient is critically important. The entire nature of the healthcare system vies against doctors being able to spend time with their patients. Health maintenance organizations rarely allow for it. Doctors' costs continue to spiral.

So, which doctors make time for chronic pain sufferers?

No rule of thumb answers this question. A doctor in a teaching hospital might give you the time you need. A doctor in private practice might. Ultimately, as explored in the Afterword of this book, different kinds of healthcare practitioners are needed to aid the cause of chronic pain. Minimally, there is an overwhelming need for a board-certified chronic pain doctor and for nurse practitioners with a chronic pain specialty.

REFERRALS FROM LAY PEOPLE ARE USEFUL BUT DIFFICULT TO COME BY

The incidence of chronic pain disease is so high, it would seem relatively easy to find a friend, relative or acquaintance who can refer you to a good healthcare practitioner. But unless you're a member of a chronic pain support group, it is difficult to get a referral from a lay person. The biggest reason for this difficulty is that success stories are relatively hard to come by. Most chronic pain sufferers start making the rounds, and years later, are still stuck in a closed loop to hell and back. Even if you get a referral, it may be impossible for that healthcare practitioner to find the time to fit in another chronic pain sufferer. Nevertheless, it's definitely worth your while to try to get a referral from someone who has been helped in a major way. There is one caveat here: avoid, for the most part, practitioners who use one treatment only – just medication or just acupuncture, for example. They seldom work, and when they do, their effectiveness rarely lasts. Beware, too, of fads or sweeping claims for success. Gravity-inversion (treatment that has you in an upside-down posture), DMSO and pyramids have come and gone, without proving themselves in the long-run as major weapons against chronic pain. If you hear about a treatment or a practitioner who claims a 100 per cent success rate, duck and run.

ALTERNATIVE PRACTITIONERS AS CO-ORDINATORS

If you find a non-medical doctor to help you in your fight against chronic pain, stick with that person and rejoice. But don't expect much in the way of further referrals. The survey for this book shows that non-physicians tend not to refer patients to other kinds of healers, even when asked. Ironically, in spite of physicians' reputed resistance to making referrals to alternative practitioners, they do it on a regular basis. For example, a chiropractor is far less likely to refer you to a physician for chronic pain, than a physician is likely to refer you to a chiropractor.

BEING YOUR OWN CHRONIC PAIN CO-ORDINATOR

The good news, and the bad, is that you ultimately have to be your own best chronic-pain co-ordinator. This is good news because you can feel empowered and less helpless when you play an important role in working out your own multi-faceted path to recovery.

This is bad news if chronic pain has plagued you for a long time, because it's terribly difficult to find the inner strength to gird up for taking co-responsibility for your progress. It's a tall, slippery mountain to climb and the echo of the mountain sounds like this: "I've tried very hard for a long time to find help, and I still haven't found it."

Recovering from chronic pain isn't as simple as merely believing in wellness. But if you don't have at least a kernel of faith that wellness is possible, a kind of paralysis sets in. You may find yourself wondering, "Why try again? I've done my best and nothing works." Or you may find yourself stuck with the thought, "I've been in too much pain, for too long, to make it back to a good life."

This kind of pessimism is to be expected. Chronic pain breeds pessimism as surely as love begets joy. The good news is that you can get well in spite of your painful past and your doubts.

The entire content of this book has been based on the successful results of people just like you. Not one, not a single individual in the group of 1,000 had an optimistic notion about recovery at their lowest point. So, if you can believe in nothing else, believe in their success. What the survey participants for this book know – their insights and knowledge – can make you well. And, with any luck at all, what you learn from them *will* help you to find a more active and pain-free existence.

The final chapters of this book will give you the additional input you need to become your own savvy co-ordinator of chronic pain practitioners and treatments. Integrate what you learn with what you know, instinctively, to be true of *your* particular chronic pain condition. And find the new level of comfort and activity that you've been seeking.

14

Healthcare Practitioners: Who to See, Who to Avoid

If you know you have chronic pain, and if you're not getting enough help to turn you life around, what kind of healthcare practitioner might you see? Or, if you have had ongoing pain for a few months or longer, and you don't feel confident that you've been adequately diagnosed, where might you find diagnostic help, and be directed toward a useful form of treatment?

Until now, chronic pain sufferers have lacked guidance to evaluate the different kinds of healthcare practitioners for their relative effectiveness in diagnosing and treating chronic pain. This chapter attempts to provide such a guide. However, because there are so many different kinds of alternative healthcare practitioners, it han't been possible to evaluate all of them. Please note that a fuller description of these therapies and what they involve is given in chapter 15.

In the section that follows, you will be told the number of survey participants who rated a particular kind of practitioner. When these numbers are relatively large – 100 or more survey participants – you can be confident of the conclusions reached. When the numbers are smaller, you will at least be able to gain meaningful insights to guide you.

ACUPUNCTURISTS
Who they are. About 75 per cent of the acupuncturists reported on in this survey are US physicians with specific training in acupuncture. The remainder represent a wide range of specialties – from nurses to physical therapists to doctors from other countries.

Number of acupuncturists in this survey: 21.

Ratings
Long-term relief: 36 per cent
Six months to two years of pain relief: 15 per cent
More than two years of pain relief: 21 per cent
Short-term relief: 25 per cent
Ineffective but not harmful: 61 per cent
Harmful: 0 per cent

What survey participants want you to know. Acupuncturists are worth trying. Most have a high level of humility about their work that you don't always find in mainstream healthcare professions. Most are accustomed to working with the most ravaging and intractable forms of pain, and take a compassionate and hopeful stance toward helping you find relief. Acupuncturists tend to be seen after pain has become chronic – a haven for those desperate with making the rounds and dizzy from hearing every diagnosis under the sun.

How to select an acupuncturist. Word of mouth is best. Some are known for their excellent results for a wide variety of problems. Others are noted for helping with a few specific kinds of ailments. Acupuncture is as much an art form as a taught skill, and when you get right down to it, you're looking for an artist who gets results regardless of training or specialty.

Notable quote. "I hadn't felt an iota of hope for five years. My condition deteriorated gradually until I was ready to quit. The doctor who gave me acupuncture saved my life by a combination of factors. His needles helped considerably. His talking to me, his encouragement, his suggestions about exercise, his confidence that I would get well all helped enormously."

BIOFEEDBACK SPECIALISTS
Who they are. Most of the well-trained biofeedback specialists in this survey are psychiatrists or psychologists who combined biofeedback lessons with mental-health therapy.

Number of biofeedback specialists in this survey: 24

Ratings
Long-term relief: 64 per cent
Six months to two years of pain relief: 20 per cent
More than two years of pain relief: 44 per cent
Short-term relief: 12 per cent
Ineffective but not harmful: 24 per cent
Harmful: 0 per cent

What survey participants want you to know. The techniques and the machinery of biofeedback vary as much as the clouds in the sky from day to day. *But biofeedback is one of the most effective and least invasive approaches to chronic pain reported on in this survey.* Some survey participants who had successful experiences resisted trying biofeedback for years. Why? They felt as if they were in a double-bind: if the treatment worked, they would feel as if the pain had been "all in their heads". If the treatment didn't work, they would feel like fools for hooking themselves up to a machine in the hope that their minds could learn to ease their pain.

Working with a practitioner you like is a huge factor in the achievement of pain relief from biofeedback. In fact, no one in this survey had any success working with someone they couldn't "talk to". Whereas it might not matter at all whether you like the neurosurgeon who can excise your brain tumour, it matters mightily that you can relax and feel comfortable with a biofeedback specialist.

How to select a biofeedback specialist. The best in this survey, by far, were medical doctors with a psychiatric specialty. Yet these were precisely the people that patients feared most going to, as if a "psychiatrist" was one step further down the road of mental illness after a "psychologist". Not so of course. Being of sound mind, but aching body, qualifies you to see a psychiatrist who is skilled in biofeedback! So ask around and try not to feel awkward about doing so. No one seems to have trouble asking professionals or lay people for a recommendation about an acupuncturist, but most survey participants were reluctant to ask their doctors or their friends for a referral to a biofeedback specialist. The biofeedback specialist, however unpublicized, is one of the few professionals in this survey who has had long-term success with a majority of chronic pain sufferers.

Notable quote. "I'm not sure if biofeedback alone works, but I am confident that almost anyone can benefit from biofeedback combined with some talk with a psychiatrist. The good thing is that psychiatrists who believe in biofeedback tend to be open-minded about your pain, and are willing to work with you on different levels. When I was first hooked to a biofeedback machine, I felt that success would mean that my mind had caused the pain in the first place. It's important to keep in mind that your mind is in pain **as a result of** your body being in pain and that biofeedback can ease this added burden of pain."

CHIROPRACTORS
Who they are. A medical specialty with at least six years of college and internship training. The focus is spinal manipulation to prevent and treat a wide range of ailments. Techniques differ widely, as does the full arsenal of treatments used, including manipulation, heat, electric stimulation, nutrition and exercise advice. Unlike medical doctors, most chiropractors recommend regular and ongoing care, as opposed to seeing a patient only when there's a problem or for an annual check-up.

Time was when chiropractors were hard-pressed to be in the mainstream of healthcare. That's changed now. The fight waged by medical doctors to dismiss chiropractors as unworthy has been lost. Many chiropractors are able to treat their patients in hospitals. Mainstream insurance companies often cover chiropractic care. It is no longer uncommon, though it is not yet the norm, for physicians to recommend chiropractors to their patients.

Number of chiropractors in this survey: 275

Ratings
Long-term relief: 40 per cent
Six months to two years of pain relief: 18 per cent
More than two years of pain relief: 22 per cent
Short-term relief: 35 per cent

Ineffective but not harmful: 13 per cent

Harmful: 12 per cent (chief cause of harm: added pain from manipulation).

What survey participants want to know. There are two very distinct camps of chronic pain sufferers ministered by chiropractors.

First, there are those who see chiropractors on a regular basis over time, and are convinced of their overall healing powers. These individuals often bring along their spouses and children for regular chiropractic care. Chiropractors, especially those who use gentle manipulative methods and a battery of other treatments, have their share of success in easing chronic pain. The greater the variety of treatments they offer, in addition to manipulation, the better they tend to do.

Second, there are people who try chiropractic treatment for a few sessions, dodn't feel better, and conclude that chiropractors have nothing to offer chronic pain sufferers. The biggest complaint from these individuals is that too many chiropractors use manipulation for chronic pain the same way they would use it for anything else, and that almost all the chiropractors assume that the source of pain is the spine, whether or not that's a reality.

How to select a chiropractor. Survey participants suggest that you ask your doctor for a referral. If he or she doesn't value chiropractic care, ask your insurance company (USA) or find out the name of a professional chiropractic association or body that can send you a list of recommended names to choose from in your area. Since debilitating chronic pain must be treated with the greatest respect, i.e. gently, it is strongly recommended that you seek out a chiropractor who uses "non-force" methods.

Notable quote. "I once read that infants who aren't held enough die from lack of touch. It makes me wonder if anyone realizes or has researched the hands-on power of the chiropractor, regardless of whatever the specific healing value of spinal manipulation might be. No matter, I found the long-term care I got from my chiropractor, a woman, both incredibly comforting and relieving of pain. The treatment is expensive, with once-a-week visits, but it has changed my life for the better, and I would be lost without it."

HOMEOPATHS

Who they are. All but one of the homeopaths mentioned in the survey for this book are medical doctors who have incorporated the specialty of homeopathic treatment into their training and practice, so we can only evaluate them. There are also homeopaths who don't have advanced degrees. Most, however, have initially trained as physicians, osteopaths or naturopaths.

The old cliché about homeopaths – that they treat you with "a hair of the dog that bit you" – is one way of understanding the homeopathic approach. Another popular phrase about this approach is "like cures like". This means that a tiny diluted amount of what would give a healthy person symptoms of illness will make a sick person well. In addition, attention is given to the individual's "constitutional" state, or the overall status of their condition. Prescriptions for homeopathic remedies are written with both the specific complaint, and the overall condition, in mind.

Number of homeopaths in this survey: 8

Ratings
Long-term relief: 75 per cent
Six months to two years of pain relief: 50 per cent
More than two years of pain relief: 25 per cent
Short-term relief: 0 per cent
Ineffective but not harmful: 25 per cent
Harmful: 0 per cent

What survey participants want you to know. Homeopaths, especially those with backgrounds as physicians or osteopaths, are unusually open-minded about chronic pain. They are holistic (believe in treating the whole person) in their approach and kind in their attitude toward chronic conditions. Homeopathy, although in existence for 200 years after its founding in Germany, is not considered "mainstream".

Therefore, for a medical doctor or osteopathic physician to study and practise homeopathy shows a willingness to look in a flexible and broad-based way at the entire physical and emotional condition of an individual with chronic pain. The homeopaths in the survey were known for their patience and persistence. If one treatment didn't work, it wasn't the patient's fault, but simply the wrong treatment. Some trial-and-error is seen as logical and inevitable by homeopaths.

Notable quote. "A homeopathic physician saved my life, with his kindness and his faith in me, not to mention his refusal to blame me or to give up. I found it comforting to work with a doctor who saw the whole person, didn't think of regular prescription drugs as a first resort and had a wide range of training and treatments to choose from. In a sense, I think that *everyone* with chronic pain should see a homeopath. They won't hurt you, and they just may have the answer for you."

KINESIOLOGISTS
Who they are. Kinesiology is the study of the mechanics and anatomy of movement. Of the seventeen kinesiologists in this survey, sixteen were chiropractors with advanced training, and one was a PhD professor who treated a chronic pain sufferer. In theory at least, kinesiologists, with their knowledge of movement, something that all chronic pain sufferers have trouble with, are the answer to a chronic pain sufferer's prayers. But there are a relatively small number of kinesiologists and a paucity of information and documented research about this specialty.

All of the kinesiologists in this survey treated or were consulted by chronic pain sufferers who had at least three years of pain and limitations, and had been to at least six other kinds of practitioners. These kinesiologists were doctors of last resort, asked to help resolve the most intractable and yielding kinds of chronic pain. To their credit, they did well! For the most part, kinesiologists use techniques similar to chiropractors. It is their perspective and learning about body movement that distinguishes them from the rest of the healthcare field.

Number of kinesiologists in this survey: 20

Ratings
Long-term relief: 50 per cent
Six months to two years of pain relief: 25 per cent
More than two years of pain relief: 25 per cent
Short-term relief: 25 per cent
Ineffective but not harmful: 25 per cent
Harmful: 0 per cent

What survey participants want you to know. Survey participants, for the very most part, want the world to know about this
little-known specialty. They are highly enthusiastic and eager
to recommend kinesiologists by name. They also want to make
sure that you're seeing a kinesologist with a qualification or an
actual degree in kinesioogy, as opposed to a practitioner who
may say that he or she "uses kinesiology".

Notable quote. "I was all but entirely crippled for seven years,
and given up on by everyone I saw – and I had just about given
up on myself – until I went to a kinesiologist. For once I wasn't
confronted with an attitude like, 'If you can't prove what you
have, and if I can't find out exactly what's wrong with you and
assign it a fancy name, then you don't really have it.' I felt like all
of my symptoms and painful times were 'expected' in a sense by
the kinesiologist. I felt like my condition wasn't oddball, but
fairly commonplace, which chronic pain is! I was par for the
course, so to speak, instead of a maniac who had nothing wrong.
I felt as if I were in the hands of a chronic pain specialist who was
going to make me well because that's what her training was
about. And that's exactly what happened – I got well.

MENTAL-HEALTH PRACTITIONERS
Who are they. Psychiatrists are medical doctors with additional
training in the treatment of mental and emotional illnesses and
addictions. They can treat chronic pain with "talk therapy,"
drug therapy and other means such as biofeedback.
Psychologists or psychotherapists are mental-health specialists
who do not have medical degrees, and who may or may not

have more training and skill in psychotherapy than psychiatrists. The training, skills and approaches of psychologists vary almost as widely as human fingerprints.

Number of mental-health practitioners in this survey: 20

Ratings
Long-term relief: 40 per cent
Six months to two years of pain relief: 0 per cent
More than two years of pain relief: 40 per cent
Short-term relief: 0 per cent
Ineffective but not harmful: 60 per cent
Harmful: 0 per cent

What survey participants want you to know. There is no such thing as a "chronic pain psychotherapist". You can find a marital counsellor, a grief counsellor, a sex therapist and a drug and alcohol counsellor, but not a chronic pain counsellor. Even though chronic pain is one of the single greatest causes of mental pain, there is no specialist for treating this condition. Survey participants were stunned to learn that the mental-health practitioners they worked with, with the exception of therapists employed in pain centres, had never talked to a chronic pain sufferer. Compassion and excellent listening skills are what matter most in choosing a mental-health practitioner. Specialized training hardly matters, since few if any mental-health practitioners have any specific and extensive training in chronic pain, although a therapist trained in grief counseling may have an edge in dealing with chronic pain.

Notable quote. "I have an Afro-American friend who once told me that she didn't want to see a white therapist, because he didn't want to have to explain the experience of being Black. I never understood what she meant until I went to see a psychologist and felt like a Martian who had to explain what Mars was like. I started to feel like a whiner, like I was being defensive, like I had experienced something beyond the therapist's realm. Still, I imagine that just having a good listener, a kind listener, maybe someone with a bit of experience in grief counseling or something like that, would be a good thing."

NATUROPATHS

Who are they. Whether a mode of healing is a year old, a hundred years old or thousands of years old, naturopaths may claim it for their arsenal of treatments. The underlying philosophy of naturopathy is to look for ways to help the body's own healing powers. Causes of ailments, not symptoms, are the focus. The Western physician's dictum of "do no harm" is interpreted by naturopaths to mean that no drugs with potential side-effects, and no surgery, with its potential for harm, should be used except as a last resort.

A plus for chronic pain sufferers is the focus that doctors of naturopathy (ND) put on how we live. They believe that the way you live – including the physical and psychological aspects of life – can affect your disease and its prevention. Naturopaths have four years of training – two in the sciences, and two in healing therapies. The majority of American states do not allow naturopathic doctors to be licensed healthcare practitioners, although some private insurance policies include naturopaths.

Number of naturopaths in this survey: 10

Ratings
Long-term relief: 60 per cent
Six months to two years of pain relief: 40 per cent
More than two years of pain relief: 20 per cent
Short-term relief: 20 per cent
Ineffective but not harmful: 20 per cent
Harmful: 0 per cent

What survey participants want you to know. With such a wide range of treatments to choose from – from herbs to exercise, massage to stress-reduction techniques – the naturopath who has an intuitive brilliance for individual patient needs, and a "feel" for which treatments might help, is bound to be helpful. Word of mouth is by far and away the best way to find a competent doctor of naturopathy.

Notable quote. "Any doctor who cares tremendously about your lifestyle, and how your lifestyle affects what's wrong with you, is a good doctor to see. I learned a lot about myself just from the many questions my naturopath asked me in the first meeting. Two of his questions: 'Do you feel worse when you're tired or under stress?' and 'What makes you feel better?' helped the two of us to work out a day-to-night course of treatment for my chronic pain."

NEUROLOGISTS

Who they are. These medical doctors specialize in all that can go wrong with the labyrinthine complexities and mysteries of the nervous system, including the brain and spine. The key word here is "mysteries", because neurologists live with the unknown day in and day out. No doubt that is why other medical specialists bring them in as consultants and gurus of last resort for anything that might be "neurological" or "neuro-muscular".

However, most chronic pain sufferers don't see neurologists because most primary care physicians don't refer them to neurologists. They should. Neurologists are sleuths, and the good ones probably love the mysteries almost as much as the solutions. They are like orchestra conductors who can deal with sections out of sync and parts needing a catalyst in order to restore harmonious function.

Number of neurologists in this survey: 40

Ratings
Long-term relief: 48 per cent
Six months to two years of pain relief: 10 per cent
More than two years of pain relief: 38 per cent
Short-term relief: 4 per cent
Ineffective but not harmful: 42 per cent
Harmful: 6 per cent (chief cause of harm: adverse effects of prescription drugs).

What survey participants want you to know. Opinions about neurologists fall into two basic categories. Patients who benefited from seeing a neurologist felt that these doctors spend more time with them, take a more thorough history and accept the reality that much about pain is still unknown. Patients who are unhappy with neurologists feel that they are too quick to write a prescription and too slow to ask about or consider lifestyle elements, including exercise and stress. A majority of survey participants mentioned being unusually nervous and wary about seeing neurologists, mostly because they were anxious about what these specialists did or what they might find wrong.

Notable quote. "I would sum up my experience with a neurologist by saying he took me seriously, and until I saw him, no doctor had. My neurologist was quick to assure me that he believed something was wrong, or else I wouldn't be there. He didn't need proof from tests; he was just accepting that things go wrong and that people with unfathomable troubles are the ones who especially need help."

NURSE PRACTITIONERS
Who they are. Whether the doctor is in and busy, or out of the office, these highly trained nurses, some of whom practise on their own, see a lot of patients with different kinds of pain. Nurse practitioners tend to be skilled, compassionate and willing to use a wide range of treatments for chronic pain, from exercise to stress-reduction, from lifestyle changes to prescription drugs.

Number of nurse practitioners in this survey: 83

Ratings
Long-term relief: 50 per cent
Six months to two years of pain relief: 10 per cent
More than two years of pain relief: 40 per cent
Short-term relief: 30 per cent
Ineffective but not harmful: 10 per cent
Harmful: 10 per cent (chief cause of harm: adverse effects of prescription drugs).

What survey participants want you to kow. It is a point of pride among nurse practitioners that they generally have better interpersonal skills than doctors, and that this ability to talk to patients and see the whole picture of a patient's life enables them to be better healers for many illnesses and afflictions, including chronic pain. The nitty-gritty of recovery from chronic pain – a gradual pace, exercise, making yourself top priority – seems obvious and important to nurse practitioners.

Notable quote. "I was in desperate shape after months of pain when I went to see my primary care doctor. When he wasn't in the office because of an emergency, I was almost in tears. Then I spent almost an hour with the nurse practitioner and now I specifically ask to see her when I make appointments. She put me back on track through a gentle approach to progress and some good basic exercises."

ORTHOPEDISTS

Who they are. Wherever it hurts when you have chronic pain – bones, joints, muscles, tendons or ligaments – it's comforting to know, at least in theory, that the orthopedist has the training and focus to help you deal with these aching parts. In practice, if what ails you shows up on an X-ray, or on an MRI scan, the chances are that an orthopedist will work with you and help you to find a way out of pain. If you have a wrecked knee, for example, an orthopedist can be a miracle-maker as a surgeon. The catch for chronic pain sufferers is that the source of chronic pain rarely shows up on a diagnostic test. That is why chronic pain is often referred to as "inexplicable" – something which cannot be precisely explained. Sad to say, when orthopedists cannot spot a tangible reason for your pain, the majority of them are dismissive and blaming, coiners of the beat-on-your-head phrase, "There's nothing really wrong with you."

Number of orthopedists in this survey: 350

Ratings
Long-term relief: 20 per cent
Six months to two years of pain relief: 15 per cent
More than two years of pain relief: 5 per cent
Short-term relief: 20 per cent
Ineffective but not harmful: 60 per cent
Harmful: 0 per cent

What survey participants want you to know. Try to avoid seeing orthopedists who believe that if the cause of pain doesn't show up on a battery of tests, either it isn't real or cannot be treated. Most patients who saw orthopedists were referred by primary care physicians who fail to grasp the distinction between the great work that orthopedists do with tangible problems, such as hip replacements, and what it takes to deal with the intangible and multi-faceted aspects of chronic pain. On the other hand, if you are referred to an orthopedist who has been shown to work well with chronic pain sufferers, seize the opportunity to work him or her.

Notable quote. "I saw two orthopedists. The first was surgery oriented, but since I had nothing to operate on, he didn't seem interested, except to prescribe an anti-inflammatory pill. But the second orthopedist helped me to get well. He worked with me on exercises, and even got down on the floor with me to show me how to do these exercises right. He also gave me breathing exercises to help reduce stress, and talked to me about the idea of gradual progress, rather than getting back all at once."

OSTEOPATHS
Who they are. Osteopaths are physicians by another name – more formally known in the USA as "osteopathic physicians" – with an orientation toward spinal manipulation and holistic healing. Osteopaths believe in correcting problems with the musculoskeletal system as a way to achieve better health. They have their own medical colleges, internships and specialties. Their knowledge, diagnostic skills and treatment skills are essentially the same as traditional physicians, but they have a greater appreciation of how our lifestyles affect our well-being.

Number of osteopaths in this survey: 98

Ratings
Long-term relief: 38 per cent
Six months to two years of pain relief: 10 per cent
More than two years of pain relief: 28 per cent
Short-term relief: 42 per cent

Ineffective but not harmful: 18 per cent
Harmful: 2 per cent (chief cause of harm: added pain from manipulation).

What survey participants want you to know. Osteopaths tend to show a real interest in their patients' lives, and this alone enables them to work well with patients who have difficult and complex pain patterns. Their training in manipulation, which tends to ease chronic pain temporarily, offers a plus to chronic pain sufferers. Osteopaths also prescribe drugs. According to survey participants, they may be more reluctant than medical doctors to make referrals to other practitioners who can help with chronic pain.

Notable quote. "I think that osteopaths are showing regular doctors the way to be. My osteopath deals more with the whole person and, this may sound strange, but he isn't afraid to touch you like most doctors are. The body is a more normal thing to him, not something to just check with machines. I got well from a whole battery of treatments that my osteopath orchestrated. I took vitamins and did exercises, and was manipulated weekly, and worked my way back from mostly in bed to being very well."

PAIN-CENTRE AND PAIN-CLINIC PRACTITIONERS
Who they are. This is our "Heinz" category – maybe not 57 varieties of healthcare practitioners, but a wide variety. Most pain centres (usually in-patient care) and pain clinics (usually out-patient care) take a multidisciplinary approach to treating chronic pain. Specialists who work at pain centres and pain clinics include, but are not limited to: neurologists, anaesthesiologists, orthopedists, physiatrists, psychiatrists, psychologists, nurses, physical therapists and occupation therapists.

Number of pain centres and pain clinics in this survey: 99

Ratings
Long-term relief: 40 per cent
Six months to two years of pain relief: 6 per cent
More than two years of pain relief: 34 per cent

Short-term relief: 40 per cent
Ineffective but not harmful: 10 per cent
Harmful: 10 per cent (chief cause of harm: patients who didn't improve felt that they were to blame. Some became depressed, assumed that recovery was impossible and stopped trying).

What survey participants want you to know. For many reasons, going to a pain centre or pain clinic can cause a lot of anxiety. There is no single model that pain centres follow; general hospitals are much more consistent in their approach to diagnosis and treatments. A pain clinic may emphasize using drug treatment or it may emphasize avoiding them. It may believe in patient empowerment or it may believe in "curing" the patient. It may use the latest technological innovations or it may concentrate on basics. It may take a centralized approach, with the director having a say in all aspects of treatment – or it may be more decentralized and chaotic. A visit to a pain centre can be fraught with anxiety because it may make you feel as if "you have to make it here or you're doomed."

Notable quote. "I got all the help I needed from a pain clinic. My only negative feeling is the wish that it hadn't taken five years for a doctor to refer me to this kind of special place. Actually, pain centres had been mentioned to me by a few doctors, but I had heard negative things about them from lay people. From my viewpoint, though, you want to be working with a *team* of experts when you have chronic pain. I had prescription drugs prescribed that helped me in the short run. I had a physical therapist who worked with me steadily. I also talked to a psychotherapist. Although I was reluctant to do so at first, because I felt it was an admission that I had head problems, I found it very useful to express myself to someone understanding about the fears and depression associated with pain."

PODIATRISTS
Who they are. Treating problems involved with the foot and ankle, including the Achilles tendon, are the province of the podiatrist. Podiatrists perform surgery, prescribe drugs, create

orthotics (corrective forms to put inside your shoes), correct malformations and work in a myriad other ways on foot and ankle disorders.

Number of podiatrists in this survey: 47

Ratings
Long-term relief: 44 per cent
Six months to two years of pain relief: 4 per cent
More than two years of pain relief: 40 per cent
Short-term relief: 4 per cent
Ineffective but not harmful: 56 per cent
Harmful: 0 per cent

What survey participants want you to know. Most chronic pain sufferers don't have pain in their feet. Instead, they see podiatrists in the hope that treatment for their feet will help other parts of their bodies. For example, if one leg is substantially shorter than the other, a corrective shoe or orthotic can relieve pain in the hips, buttocks and back. When a foot problem causes people to favour one side, care from a podiatrist can halt chronic pain in its tracks. When walking in high heels tightens the calf muscles and leads to generalized pain, advice from a podiatrist can work wonders.

Notable quote. "Over seven years of having chronic pain, I was treated like a malingerer and chronic whiner. I lost my job, my marriage and the affection of my children. I was drinking at a party one night, and telling a stranger about my years of pain, when he suggested I come to his office the next day for a free consultation. He diagnosed me with short-leg syndrome and prescribed an orthotic to put into one of my shoes. One week later, I had no more pain. *I actually had no more pain.* This was, and remains, a miracle to me."

PHYSIATRISTS
Who they are. Sometimes called Doctors of Physical and Rehabilitative Medicine, physiatrists are medical doctors with a specialty in helping the disabled and injured to restore their

lives to maximum functioning. They use virtually every means available to bring about this restoration, from prescribed exercise routines to heat and electrical stimulation, from injections into muscles to prescription drugs (only when absolutely necessary) to physical therapy.

Number of physiatrists in this survey: 80

Ratings
Long-term relief: 60 per cent
Six months to two years of pain relief: 4 per cent
More than two years of pain relief: 56 per cent
Short-term relief: 28 per cent
Ineffective but not harmful: 10 per cent
Harmful: 2 per cent (chief cause of harm: "triggerpoint injections" – injections into painful areas of muscles).

What survey participants want you to know. If there is a consistent miracle worker for chronic pain sufferers, according to survey participants, it is the physiatrist, or doctor of physical and rehabilitative medicine. When you're in great pain over months and years, it is like having been in a train wreck – the equivalent of being banged up everywhere, out of sync, unable to get different parts of the body working fluidly. The physiatrist is accustomed to working with major injuries and incapacitation.

Notable quote. "The only problem with a 'physiatrist' is people thinking I said 'psychiatrist'. You're talking about a miracle worker here. Not only was I put back together again, with my working as a true partner in the physical therapy, but I saw people I thought would never function again come back to life under the physiatrist's care. This is a Doctor for the Disabled. People should look for one, call their local medical societies, go online, ask friends, check with their doctors . . . but find one and see one."

PHYSICAL THERAPISTS
Who they are. Physical therapists are non-medical doctors with advanced training in working with all kinds of physical disabil-

ities and showing people how to move and exercise their way back to maximum functioning. Physical therapists are accustomed to working with broken bodies, and the injured states of mind that often come with the territory.

Number of physical therapists in this survey: 230

Ratings
Long-term relief: 44 per cent
Six months to two years of pain relief: 12 per cent
More than two years of pain relief: 32 per cent
Short-term relief: 28 per cent
Ineffective but not harmful: 24 per cent
Harmful: 4 per cent (chief cause of harm: movements or exercise that made matters worse).

What survey participants want you to know. Physical therapy at its best is a set of skills with an intuitive human being behind them. It is this intuition as much as the skills that shapes the therapy and, ultimately, gives hope to the patient. The best physical therapists have a great respect for pain, and simultaneously, a real determination to help you get through it. They are a mixture of teacher, taskmaster and motivator. One relatively minor note of caution: some physical therapists are accustomed to working only with the instances of pain where pain is a prerequisite for gain. For example, if you are recovering from shoulder surgery, for example, some pain in your rehabilitation is unavoidable. In working with chronic pain sufferers, it is occasionally difficult for physical therapists to realize that increases in pain level, or proceeding too quickly, can be harmful.

Notable quote. "In my mind, physical therapists are pain specialists. I would recommend that everyone see one. If you don't, you're missing an obviously good bet."

PRIMARY CARE PRACTITIONERS*
Who they are. Also referred to as "general practitioners" and "family doctors", primary care practitioners are frequently the first doctor that chronic pain sufferers see, often when their

pain is recently onset and not yet classified as "chronic". Their diagnostic skills, and ability to refer to the right specialist when needed, are critical to the outcome of chronic pain. The buck doesn't stop with them, but their judgement often determines where acute pain ends and chronic pain begins.

*For our purposes, internists, a separate specialty, are included in this category.

Number of general practitioners in this survey: 461

Ratings
Long-term relief: 12 per cent
Six months to two years of pain relief: 3 per cent
More than two years of pain relief: 9 per cent
Short-term relief: 30 per cent
Ineffective but not harmful: 54 per cent
Harmful: 4 per cent (chief cause of harm: adverse effect of prescription drugs).

What survey participants want you to know. There is nothing as helpful to a chronic pain sufferer than to have the treatment of pain start and end with their "regular doctor". This is the doctor they often know best and can talk to most comfortably. More people see general practitioners than any other kind of healthcare practitioner. Unfortunately, the experience tends to be fruitless for preventing or resolving chronic pain.

Notable quote. "I could sense my doctor's frustration about my worsening condition. The longer the pain lasted, the more drug treatments that failed, the more concerned he became, and the more agitated. I wound up feeling as sorry for him as I did for myself. Family doctors are supposed to know a lot about everything, but I don't think they know nearly enough about chronic pain."

YOGA TEACHERS
Who they are. Yoga instructors are every conceivable manner of individual with every possible level of schooling. In spite of this lack of standards – virtually anyone in this world who wants to teach yoga can – yoga insructors succeed relatively

well with chronic pain sufferers. Please note that yoga teachers don't simply teach "yoga exercises", they teach a state of mind, a way of thinking, a discipline, an approach to life. Although it is difficult to generalize about such a diverse group, yoga teachers tend to be calming, encouraging and filled with a powerful belief that the mind and body can move from where it is to a better place.

Number of yoga teachers in this survey: 58

Ratings
Long-term relief: 48 per cent
Six months to two years of pain relief: 12 per cent
More than two years of pain relief 36 per cent
Short-term relief: 0 per cent
Ineffective but not harmful: 44 per cent
Harmful: 8 per cent (chief cause of harm: exercises that were beyond the physical abilities of chronic pain sufferers).

What survey participants want you to know. Yoga is something of a make-or-break therapy for a chronic pain sufferer. In the hands of a yoga teacher who understands the need to go very slowly, and who has the common sense to know that many yoga exercises can be harmful to someone whose body has been hurting for a long time, yoga can help a pained body to get well. However, in the hands of a yoga teacher who has one pace – that pace being suited to someone relatively fit – yoga is risky. Referrals are critical here.

Notable quote. "My yoga teacher had never worked with anyone who had chronic pain. But she listened carefully, asked a lot of questions, and with no background at all in chronic pain, helped me to go from a near-cripple to a fully active human being again in six months. It seemed like a miracle to me then; it still seems like one now."

15

Treatments for Chronic Pain: Which Work, which Don't Work

There are more potential treatments for chronic pain that any individual could try in a lifetime. This chapter will help you to make sense of some of these treatments, using a blend of survey data and research from medical journals. For example, do chiropractic adjustments reduce chronic pain? Should muscle relaxants be prescribed for chronic pain? Are anti-inflammatories helpful? Does yoga have value? How about biofeedback? Are herbal remedies helpful? Does TENS (*see* p. 199) or PENS (*see* p. 196) work? Will magnetic therapy go the way of anti-gravity machines, pyramids and DMSO (*see* p. 189)?

POINTS TO BEAR IN MIND

1. Ratings in this chapter reflect the input of survey participants. They are informative – combining medical journal research with chronic pain sufferers' input – but they are by no means definitive. No major, definitive scientific study has ever been conducted by the medical community into the value of a wide range of treatments for chronic pain.

2. Except in rare instances, no single-treatment approach is enough to restore a chronic pain sufferer to good health. A multi-faceted approach is almost always necessary to complete the trip back to wellness.

3. Treatments rated poorly in this chapter, even those scientifically documented as utterly and totally worthless, will still

help someone with chronic pain. This positive effect of a treatment with no known value is called the placebo effect. If we take something that we think may help us, it will, about a third of the time.

Since there are more treatments to try than you have the time or money to experiment with, and since some of these treatments are downright dangerous, use this chapter as your starting point. Learn all that you can about any treatment that interests you. Let your knowledge guide the way and keep you at arm's length from risky and harmful treatment approaches.

4. Remember, please, that the ratings in this chapter give you a guide to follow, rather than hard and fast conclusions. No rating is entirely positive or negative. For example, "Excellent" might mean that a treatment worked wonders for eight out of ten people, but wasted the time and money of two out of ten people. "Poor" might mean, to cite another example, that only three out of ten people had success with a treatment, but for these people, the treatment was a blessing.

ACUPUNCTURE

Defined. Stimulation, with needles, of energy points along meridian channels. Not entirely explainable in traditional medical terms.

Overall rating. Good

How to think about acupuncture. Acupuncture is almost always worth a try for chronic pain. No matter where the pain is – hip, knee, buttock, back, elbow, shoulder or everywhere at once – acupuncture tends to help significantly about half the time. Give this modality a month's worth of treatments before you make up your mind about it. If acupuncture really works, the effect is likely to last for months or years without additional treatments.

ALEXANDER THERAPY

Defined. Postural therapy.

Overall rating. Usually of no value.

How to think about Alexander therapy. Learning to stand with your spine properly aligned is a good idea and it might have value for some chronic pain sufferers, especially those whose debilitating pain has caused them to compensate for, and change, the way they used to stand. However, of the nine chronic survey participants who tried the Alexander technique, only two felt it helped.

ALGOLOGY

Defined. A medical specialty focusing on the treatment of pain through a wide range of treatments.

Overall rating. Worth looking into.

How to think about algology. An algologist is a medical specialty that has yet to achieve major status. You won't find an "algologist" category in your local telephone directory. Still, it might well be worth your while to check with your local medical association and get the names of medical doctors who specialize in the treatment of pain. An algologist by any other name might be a neurologist, an anaesthesiologist, a family practitioner or a doctor of physical and rehabilitative medicine. Algology may hold great hope for the future, especially if more pain research is done and if the specialty is taken more seriously by the healthcare professions.

BIOFEEDBACK

Defined. The use of a computerized method to measure basic functioning rates such as heartbeat and muscle tension, with the goal of teaching you how to control these functions.

Overall rating. Good to excellent.

How to think about biofeedback. Nearly two-thirds of twenty-four survey participants in this book got long-term relief from biofeedback. Your best bet is to find a psychiatrist who can combine biofeedback with talk therapy. Think about biofeedback as a means of tapping into the sometimes magical power of our minds to heal our bodies.

BRACES AND SUPPORTS FOR BACKS

Defined. Manufactured means of keeping your back properly aligned when an injury or pain prevents your muscles from doing the job for you.

Overall rating. Fair.

How to think about braces and supports. Braces for your back are, at best, temporary measures. Do not wear them for more than a week unless you have more than one medical opinion demonstrating that the use of a brace or support is medically indicated. Your abdominal muscles act as a natural brace in keeping your spine properly aligned. Wearing a back brace prohibits you from using these muscles as fully as you would without a brace. The longer you wear a brace, the weaker your muscles get. In the short run, on occasion, back braces can ease a painful day or even prevent pain during a long and taxing day.

COLD THERAPY

Defined. The use of cold substances such as ice packs and hydrocollators to ease spasming and pain.

Overall rating. Good.

How to think about cold therapy. Chances are that not enough chronic pain sufferers derive the benefits of cold therapy, because of the rule of thumb that says you should apply cold to a painful area only up to forty-eight hours after an injury. That's a good rule for acute pain, not chronic pain.

If you're a chronic pain sufferer, the initial injury that triggered your chronic pain may have occurred years ago. Or there may never have been an injury; chronic pain may have just started and continued in a way that cannot be traced or explained. Why then use ice for chronic pain? Because it works for nearly 75 per cent of individuals who use it. When should you use it? Experiment! If you have a particular painful area that is localized, or you have spasming that is causing you pain, try cold therapy. If it doesn't feel right, stop. Never apply ice without a thin towel or fabric between you and the cold. Also, never leave ice on for more than five minutes at a time as frostbite can result from longer applications.

DMSO

Defined. An industrial solvent (dimethyl sulfoxide) used topically in a purer form by veterinarians to reduce swelling in animals. The use of DMSO as a painkiller for human beings is illegal.

Overall rating. Good (with significant risks and adverse effects).

How to think about DMSO. There's a media expression in America that "everyone gets their fifteen minutes in the spotlight." In the world of chronic pain, many substances, including an illegal substance like DMSO, seem to get their fifteen minutes and then linger much longer than that in the shadows of the nation's self-remedies. Two decades ago, the publicity for DMSO made the elixirs and claims of quacks seem tame by comparison. Many a tree was felled by publishers eager to cash in on the DMSO craze. Our conclusion about DMSO: of thirty people who used it, twenty found it of value in reducing pain and spasming. However, it also caused some unpleasant side-effects, namely a foul taste in the mouth, not to mention other potentially dangerous effects.

ELECTRICAL STIMULATION

Defined. A wide variety of machines that send different kinds of electric current into muscles in the hope of curbing spasming, relaxing muscle tension and bringing the healing benefits of increased blood flow to the area.

Overall rating. Fair.

How to think about electrical stimulation. Physical therapists, chiropractors and other practitioners use different kinds of electrical stimulation to supplement other healing forces being used. Electrical stimulation *does* work for some people and it's been used in some form for centuries without any known harmful effects.

EXERCISE

Defined. A systematic way of stretching and strengthening muscles.

Overall rating. Excellent.

How to think about exercise. Exercise is vital to your fitness, your mood, your attitude and your rate of progress. Few chronic pain sufferers resolve their pain and live active lives without exercise playing a key role in their recovery. The exercise programme in this book is worth your time and attention. Exercise programmes prescribed by experts – physiatrists and physical therapists to name two medical disciplines trained in exercise – are also worth considering. Exercise for chronic pain sufferers is different from fitness programmes. Greater fitness is an ultimate goal, but rehabilitation and recovery are the only goals worth considering at the outset. Forget "no pain, no gain." "Gain without pain" is the only logical goal.

FELDENKRAIS THERAPY

Defined. One-on-one sessions with a practitioner trained in using touch, exercise and breathing to improve your fitness and lessen your pain.

Overall rating. Fair to good.

How to think about Feldenkrais therpy. It might help you to learn more about your body and how you use it. Although specific methods are taught to practitioners of this healing approach, the artistry and interpersonal skills of the practitioner are unusually important in bringing about a successful outcome.

FITNESS TRAINING
Defined. A customized programme for achieving greater fitness.

Overall rating. Poor.

How to think about fitness training. It's best *not* to think about fitness training for the initial phase of recovery from chronic pain. The fitness instructors mentioned by this book's survey participants thought they knew how to proceed gradually, but their rate of anticipated progress was far too great for chronic pain sufferers. Additionally, their prescribed exercise routines were, overall, far too strenuous.

FOOT ORTHOTICS
Defined. A form that fits into your shoe to provide comfort and, more critically, proper "foot posture". Foot orthotics affect the alignment of your entire body.

Overall rating. Excellent.

How to think about foot orthotics. Research shows that chronic pain rarely starts in the head. To the contrary, based on the responses and miraculous successes of twenty-eight survey participants who got orthotics to help their chronic pain, this pain can start as far from the head as you can get. Conditions like flattened arches, overly high arches and short-leg syndrome can be corrected by foot orthotics. If you have any doubt at all about the role that your feet may play in your chronic pain, walk (don't run) to your nearest qualified podiatrist, sports orthopedist or sports medicine specialist. It could be that corrective measures from the bottom up might do you a world of good.

FOOT REFLEXOLOGY
Defined. Applying pressure and massage to areas of the feet that supposedly correspond to specific areas of the body, including common areas of chronic pain such as the lower back, upper back, hips and shoulders.

Overall rating. Poor to fair.

How to think about foot reflexology. It can't hurt. It may feel good. If you hear of a practitioner who has gotten good results for chronic pain sufferers, reflexology may be worth a try. If it works, expect some relief from pain in the short term, but not in the long run.

GRAVITY INVERSION

Defined. Lying upside down, or tilting downward, usually with the aid of an exercise machine, in order to reap the supposed benefits of reversing gravity.

Overall rating. Poor to fair (with negative effects from overly strenuous exercises while in an upside-down position).

How to think about gravity inversion. In its heyday, gravity inversion was touted as somewhat miraculous – with claims of slowed aging, improved digestion and reduced back pain. The theory is that our being upright, with gravity compressing our spines and other body parts, creates back pain and other ailments of the musculoskeletal system. Gravity inversion can be a good way to gently stretch the body. On the negative side, strenuous exercises or overstretching or putting the body in a position it isn't accustomed to, can lead to a worsening of chronic pain. Reversing gravity can also worsen a number of medical conditions, so talk to your healthcare practitioner before trying it.

HEAT THERAPY

Defined. The application of warmth, preferably moist heat, in order to relax muscles and increase the blood flow to areas of the body that need healing and repair.

Overall rating. Good to excellent.

How to think about heat theapy. Moist heat is soothing. That's a good start. And judiciously applied moist heat seems to speed the recovery process. Taking a warm bath when your muscles are tense or aching can literally wash away discomfort. Using a heat hydrocollator, or a heating pad with a cotton cover that can be moistened, can make you feel like you're doing something good for yourself. (Caution: Do *not* overdo a good thing. Make your bath warm, not hot. "Hot" can tire your muscles and add to pain. Prolonged exposure to hot water also can be dangerous for individuals with certain medical conditions.)

HERBAL THERAPIES

Defined. Natural substances in the form of pills, tea, compresses, food or other means of delivery.

Overall rating. Unknown.

How to think about herbal therapies. Know this for certain: you're going to hear of new miracle pain-killing foods and herbs and supplements and vitamins for the rest of your life. Vitamin C was once touted for pain. Vitamin E had its run. Chinese herbs and herbal teas have been written about widely. Today, glucosamine sulfate combined with chondroitan is helping some 50–70 per cent of individuals suffering from worn and painful knees. But, generally, in spite of the claims and acclaim for herbal therapies, there is no evidence that they do help chronic pain.

Supplements currently in the news for chronic pain include curcumin, cayenne pepper, ginger and bromelain. Curcumin is found in turmeric and is said to be an anti-inflammatory agent. Cayenne pepper contains capsaicin, which can act as a natural pain-stopper. Ginger supposedly lowers level of substance P, which is thought to be a culprit in transmitting pain and heightening inflammation. Bromelain is an enzyme found in pineapple and purportedly works on swelling and inflammation. It can't harm you to eat some pineapple every day (unless you're allergic to it!), but generally, it is strongly advised that you do *not* experiment with any herbal remedies without first consulting with a doctor or nutritionist.

HYDRATION

Defined. Drinking more water as a way to "wash away" chronic pain.

Overall rating. Unknown.

How to think about hydration. In theory, muscle activity gives off waste products. If these waste products hang around your muscles – and if your muscles don't receive a fresh ongoing supply of oxygen – you'll suffer more pain. As with numerous theories about chronic pain, this one hasn't been proven to hold water, but it's worth a try. If you aren't drinking eight eight-ounce glasses of water every day, try it.

IMPLANTED PUMPS

Defined. Technologically innovative devices surgically placed under the skin for the purpose of delivering powerful painkillers to specific areas of the body.

Overall rating. Fair to good.

How to think about implanted pumps. Delivering less painkilling medication to the body in general, and bringing more painkilling medication to a specific area of the body, is the advantage of these pumps. Relief from pain can be greater and the risk of addiction less. Anaesthesiologists and neurosurgeons, usually at pain centres, tend to be experienced with this procedure. Consider these pumps an important last-resort way to curb unyielding pain. Some patients have found them to be a godsend; others have had bad experiences.

KINESIOLOGY

Defined. The science of understanding the mechanics of how the body moves. Applied kinesiology spans the use of manipulation, exercise, posture therapy and other treatments.

Overall rating. Good to excellent.

How to think about kinesiology. Most practising kinesiologists are chiropractors. Look for a practitioner who has a degree in kinesiology.

MAGNET THERAPY

Defined. Applying magnets directly to areas of the body that hurt.

Overall rating. Fair to good.

How to think about magnet therapy. Rather than think about magnet therapy too much, you might want to simply give it a try. There is no indication that putting magnets on your skin can harm you, and there is some small but important scientific research that shows good results for different kinds of pain. If your chronic pain is generalized, or ever-shifting, this may be of use to you. But if specific parts of you hurt, magnet therapy could be worth trying.

MANIPULATION

Defined. Manually adjusting different parts of the spine to properly align the body, remove the cause of dysfunction and improve overall health.

Overall rating. Fair to good.

How to think about manipulaion. You may get short-term relief and, if you receive manipulation treatments on a regular basis, you may get significant long-term relief. Manipulation alone isn't likely to resolve years of chronic pain, but it can be one of several treatments that helps you to achieve wellness.

NERVE BLOCKS

Defined. A procedure designed to deaden parts of the nervous system thought to be causing or transmitting extreme and persistent pain. Many means of blocking pain can be used, including injections, surgery, chemicals, lasers, heat and cold.

Overall rating. Fair to good (with risks of injury from the procedure).

How to think about nerve blocks. They're a last resort. Results can be gloriously good or a complete failure with greater discomfort than you had to start with. If everything about the precise mechanisms of pain were known, nerve blocks might have a better chance of working consistently well. However, mysteries about chronic pain prevail, and even when nerve blocks work, it's not known how long the salutary effects will hold up.

PAIN CLINICS AND CENTRES

Defined. A healthcare facility devoted to the treatment of pain. Some pain clinics and centres use a multidisciplinary approach, bringing different medical specialties to bear on a long-term painful condition.

Overall rating. Fair to good.

How to think about pain centres. Multidisciplinary healthcare resources dedicated to dealing with pain should improve your odds of success. This is not necessarily the case though. Pain centres are only as good as their directors, practitioners and programmes. Your best route to selecting a good pain treatment facility is via a referral from a patient who has been helped.

PENS

Defined: PENS stands for percutaneous (under the skin) electrical nerve stimulation. An electrical current is sent through small needles inserted in areas like the lower back.

Overall rating. Fair.

How to think about PENS. It is a below-the-skin version of TENS (discussed later in this chapter). A report in the *Journal of the American Medical Association* reveals that back sufferers felt better after PENS treatments than after more common treatments for back pain. For chronic pain, consider PENS as one small part of an overall treatment, with a fair chance of getting some relief.

PHYSICAL THERAPY

Defined. Rehabilitating parts of the body through a variety of movement therapies, exercise, manipulation, heat, cold, electrical stimulation and a thorough working knowledge of an individual patient's conditions.

Overall rating. Good to excellent.

How to think about physical therapy. Physical types of therapy are essential to anyone who has physical problems – it's that simple. What isn't so simple is that many physical therapists are relatively uninformed about chronic pain and unaccustomed to working with its mysteries and complexities and the need for a more gradual approach.

PRESCRIPTION DRUGS
Defined. Prescription drugs referred to in the book are limited to three categories of drugs prescribed for pain: analgesics (pain relievers), anti-inflammatories and muscle relaxants.

Overall rating. Poor (with adverse effects ranging from mild to lethal).

How to think about prescription drugs. Typically prescribed painkillers, anti-inflammatory drugs and muscle relaxants don't work for chronic pain. They are over-prescribed without a shred of widely accepted documentation of effectiveness. It is known that all of these drugs have adverse effects, some of them extremely dangerous. On the other hand, there is an under-utilization of more potent painkillers on the baseless grounds that these drugs can be addictive. If potent painkillers can be used in the short run to help you get back on your feet in the long run, their use may be indicated. Don't be afraid to seek more than one physician's opinion about the use of powerful prescription painkillers, and keep in mind that the relatively mild ones seem to offer more bad effects than good.

PSYCHOLOGY
Defined. "Talk therapy" designed to help individuals work through the anxieties, fears, depression and negative feelings associated with chronic pain.

Overall rating. Good to excellent.

How to think about psychology. It can be useful for anyone who has had any debilitating medical problem for more than a few weeks. Graduate schools for psychology don't have a chronic pain specialty, but an excellent therapist who knows nothing about chronic pain can still be of great help.

ROLFING

Defined. Deep massage designed to restore body alignment by loosening or freeing up adhesions in the fascia (the connective tissue that covers muscles).

Overall rating. Not generally recommended for chronic pain.

How to think about rolfing. This deep form of massage, sometimes referred to as structural integration, is seemingly too painful for the vast majority of chronic pain sufferers. However, if your chronic pain is not severe, and if you're willing to endure the discomfort of a deep-tissue massage, you might find rolfing of real benefit. It takes several weeks of rolfing, at least, to determine its long-term value.

SHIATSU

Defined. A Japanese form of acupressure designed to free up energy and correct dysfunctions caused by energy blocks and imbalances.

Overall rating. Good.

How to think about shiatsu. When done more gently than usual, it can help chronic pain. Traditional shiatsu employs fingertip and thumb pressure. However, some survey participants mentioned shiatsu therapists walking on their backs. If you have chronic pain, do not allow anyone to walk on your back, no matter what claims may be made for its therapeutic value!

T'AI CHI

Defined. A form of martial arts that focuses on slow and smooth motions and body awareness.

Overall rating. Good to excellent.

How to think about T'ai Chi. It feels like a slow-movement dance while in a meditative state. "I felt like I slowly moved my body and head out of chronic pain," said one survey participant.

TENS

Defined. Transcutaneous Electric Nerve Stimulation is electrical stimulation therapy designed to reduce muscle spasming.

Overall rating. Poor to fair.

How to think about TENS. Of the forty survey participants who tried a TENS unit, only twelve found it of any value and eight found it uncomfortable. However, those who found it beneficial believed that it helped them to cut down on medications and make strides forward.

YOGA

Defined. Integration of a state of mind and a set of body positions to foster overall well-being.

Overall rating. Excellent.

How to think about yoga. It's still here and going strong after thousands of years, and for countless people worldwide it's an integral and beneficial part of their lives. The only "catch" about yoga for chronic sufferers is that many traditional yoga positions and exercises are dangerous. If you can find yourself a yoga instructor who is willing and able to customize yoga to fit your physical state, you should definitely give yoga a try.

Afterword

For hundreds of millions of people worldwide, the epidemic of chronic pain is a scandal and a tragedy. And yet no major study of chronic pain management has ever been conducted. Medical associations and research centres ought to be leading the way, but they aren't. Governments should be helping out with funding, but they're not. No one knows with any degree of certainty how many chronic pain sufferers there are, or how chronic pain might be treated or what kinds of research are most needed. In 1986, the US National Center for Health Statistics considered doing a survey about chronic pain, but it was never conducted.

In order for progress to be made in this area, medical schools must teach chronic pain management – not give a lick and a swipe to the subject in less than 0.5 per cent of their instructional time. Healthcare professionals must protest against, and work to change, the instructional training in chronic pain that the vast majority of them consider inadequate. They must argue for more research funds. They must encourage their patients to insist that health insurance organizations understand and pay for chronic pain management in a way that goes far beyond a prescription pad. It takes time to help chronic pain sufferers to get well again. To date health-insurance providers have rarely proved willing to pay for this time.

Ironically, these inadequacies in chronic pain treatment give the medical world an excellent opportunity to form a closer alliance with the public. Is there a physician alive who isn't aware of the growing skepticism and mistrust of consumers about healthcare? Is there anyone today who hasn't heard at least one joke about doctor arrogance? You probably know the classic one: God was afraid one day that He had become arrogant. Why are you afraid, an angel asked Him? I dreamed I was a doctor, replied God.

This is a difficult time for medical doctors. The costs to get trained and licensed are higher than ever. The public is more challenging. Health maintenance organizations make it tough, and sometimes impossible, to do a good job. We forget how desperately we need and want good doctors until we run to them to be healed. How wonderful it would be if doctors, with the public's backing, used chronic pain as a rallying cry to give their profession more of the tools and time needed to achieve greater excellence in all of their work.

More specifically, in order to better help chronic pain sufferers worldwide, I believe that three new kinds of healthcare specialists are needed:

1. Physicians specializing in chronic pain management. Remarkably, although there are now doctors who call themselves algologists (pain specialists), most do not have extensive, all-around training in chronic pain management, and algology is not a board-certified specialty.

2. Chronic pain counsellors. These experts would have a degree in counseling or psychotherapy, with advanced training in chronic pain management. Most, if not all, chronic pain sufferers need help with depression. All need the comfort of being understood. All need guidance about relationships, the activities of daily living and work. A chronic pain counsellor would help meet these needs.

3. Nurse practitioners with advanced training in chronic pain. These practitioners would have some of the same insights as a chronic pain counsellor, plus an extensive knowledge of medications and medical specialties.

A new and shared vision is needed. Insurance companies need to change their thinking about chronic pain. With few exceptions, they don't allow for, or pay for, the individualized and multi-faceted treatment that chronic pain sufferers require.

Medical doctors must change their thinking. The usual paradigm – diagnose the physical cause and treat it in a uniform way doesn't work for chronic pain. It is wrong to believe that because we cannot yet explain the symptoms and mechanisms of chronic pain, that its sufferers don't warrant every effort to help them.

Chronic pain must be viewed for what it is – today's most crippling health epidemic. Not "nothing really wrong." But something horribly wrong and in need of attention and progress.

Empathy, compassion and comfort must become an integral part of the medical arsenal used to treat and manage chronic pain.

Chronic pain sufferers must join forces against the misinformation and back-handed dismissals that keep them making the rounds so fruitlessly. They must empower themselves. Knowledge gained from recovered chronic pain sufferers is the key to this empowerment.

Index